colourhealinghome

MITCHELL BEAZLEY

colourhealinghome

CATHERINE CUMMING

Dedicated with love to Antony and Mary

First published in Great Britain in 2000
by Mitchell Beazley, an imprint of Octopus
Publishing Group Limited, 2–4 Heron Quays,
London E14 4JP
Reprinted 2002
Copyright © Octopus Publishing Group Limited
2000
Illustration copyright © Octopus Publishing Group
Limited 2000

Executive Editor: **Judith More**
Executive Art Editor: **Janis Utton**
Project Editor: **Selina Mumford**
Editor: **Jonathan Hilton**
Layout and Illustration Design: **Tony Spalding**
Picture Research: **Jo Walton**
Production: **Jessame Emms**
Index: **Hilary Bird**

Distributed in the United States and Canada by
Sterling Publishing Co. Inc.
387 Park Avenue South
New York, NY 10016

ISBN 1 84000 365 0

A CIP record for this book is available from
the British Library

contents

colour

andwellbeing

colourwheel

The colour wheel – on which colours are arranged in their natural order – is a traditional image used to explain the relationship between different colours and how new ones can be created. The three primary pigment colours (those that cannot be made from other colours) are red, yellow, and blue.

If you mix any two of the primary colours together you have what is known as a secondary colour: orange (red + yellow), green (yellow + blue), and violet (blue + red). When white is added to a particular colour, or hue, it is referred to as a tint. When black is added, you have a shade. Tone refers to the degree of brightness. When you are decorating your home, simply being aware of the shade and tonal value of the hues that are being used in conjunction with each other can help you to achieve just the right effect for balance and contrast.

Colours that are positioned directly opposite each other on the wheel – orange and blue, for example – are known as complementary colours. As well as being placed across from each other on the wheel, these hues are also most opposite to each other in character. When using one dominant colour in a scheme, perhaps on the walls, then the eye naturally craves the relief and balance that can be instantly achieved simply by introducing a splash of its complementary somewhere within the room.

A hue's perceived "warmth" or "coolness" is another basic concept. Colours at the red/orange end of the spectrum not only add warmth to a room, they also appear to advance toward you and so visually close down the available space. Conversely, colours at the blue/green end of the spectrum create a cool atmosphere and, because they appear to recede, produce an airy, spacious feeling.

There are many ways in which you can use these colour characteristics to advantage. In order to make a low ceiling look higher, for example, you could paint it in a light, cool colour; painting a high ceiling in a rich, warm colour will make it seem lower. Similarly, you can make the end wall of a long corridor look less distant by painting it in a warm colour, or the side walls of a narrow space less confining by painting them in a cool colour. Overall, however, decorative schemes appear more balanced when cool and warm colours are used together.

light vs pigment

Coloured light and coloured pigment are very different in the way they react when they are mixed together. The three primaries of light are red, green, and blue/violet, producing secondaries of yellow (red + green), turquoise (green + blue/violet), and magenta (red + blue/violet). If all three primaries of light are mixed together, the complete visible spectrum is assembled and white light results. However, where all three primaries of pigment coincide, black is formed. This is because each pigment reflects only the wavelengths of light corresponding to its own colour, and subtracts all the others. Although in terms of colour therapy, coloured light is far more powerful than coloured pigment, and so must be used in the home with caution and, if part of a treatment, only by a qualified practitioner, pigment colours are still potent and their effects should not be underestimated.

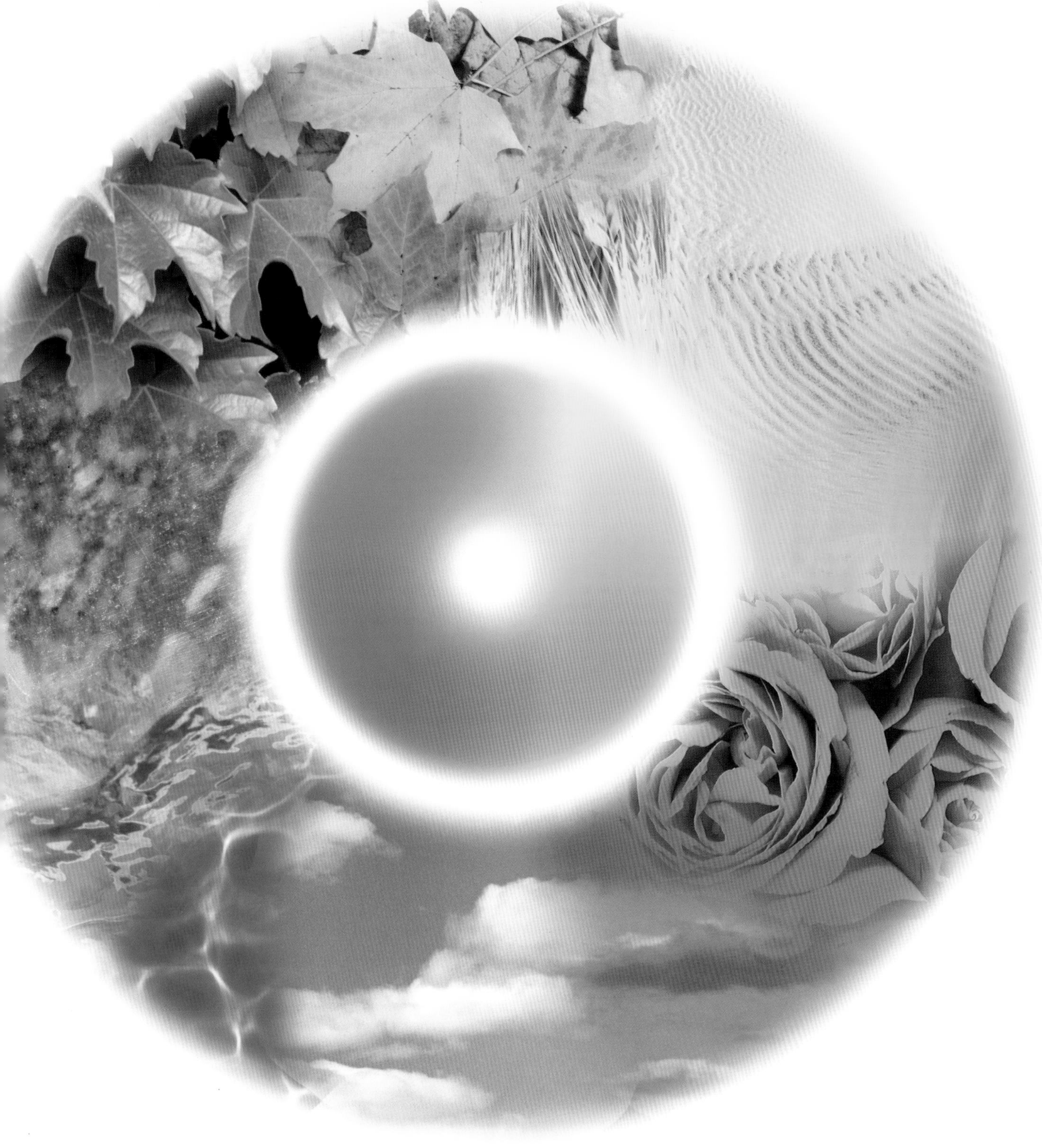

supportinghues

The pure colours of the rainbow are the most nourishing and replenishing, each emitting its own unique vibration of life, of health, and of healing. The other colours around us, however, should not be discounted as they, too, have their place in steadying and supporting our vibrant world of colour.

White light is an amalgam – all hues and yet none at all (*see pp. 8–9*). Strictly speaking, white is not a colour – rather, it is an absence of colour. Yet in terms of colour therapy, white is associated with light, purity, and grace. It is clean, tranquil, and innocent. In the home setting, white often provides the perfect background for a range of other colours such as those found in furniture, wall paintings, flooring, and decorative motifs and themes. However, if white is used indiscriminately, without sufficient relief, it can make your home feel empty, sterile, and even isolating.

cautionary black

The opposite of white is black – a colour that is best treated with caution in a home decorative scheme unless it is applied in small quantities, and alongside other colours for balance.

Reflecting none of the colour components of light, black is absorbent and so can be draining and negative in its effect. If you dress in black, it is best to offset its influence by wearing coloured accessories. Black tends to be worn more often by people living or working in city settings –

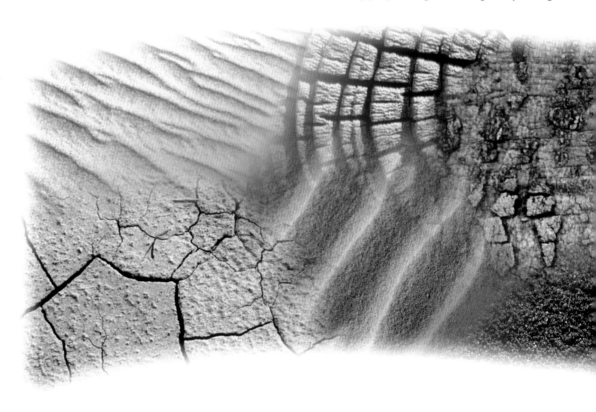

perhaps because black is sometimes thought to be protective in nature. However, it is not a healthy colour as it does not transmit light, allowing no colours through to the skin. Because of this, black does not nourish us in any way unlike the other hues which let light pass through them.

supportive gray

White pigment when it is mixed with black forms gray. This is a neutral colour, neither hot nor cold. Because when gray is used by itself it feels flat and lifeless, this colour is often considered to be negative in effect, yet it provides enormous support to the other hues.

An environment that contains no gray can sometimes seem to lack solidity and structure. Any colour of the rainbow is enhanced and supported by the presence of gray, but it is not a healthy choice of colour for an overall interior decorative scheme. However, if it is used in association with the more vibrant hues, then gray can be extremely helpful.

colours of nature

The range of browns are grounding, supportive, and earthy colours. Brown is the colour of commitment, and there is a wide range of natural browns commonly found in such domestic objects as wooden furniture as well as wooden flooring, doors, window frames, and so on. Like the earthy tones of nature, browns tend to be perceived as warm and inviting in character. Combining brown with certain other colours forms earthy, softer versions of the original hues. This mixing of colours works best with warm hues, such as the reds and oranges.

As a general rule, be guided by the fact that the purer the hue, the healthier its effect on you tends to be. Surrounding yourself with too many murky tones could reflect and generate confusion or depression and should, therefore, be relieved by the inclusion of lighter, brighter colours. An attraction to a particularly pure, clear hue often denotes a clarity and confidence with the issues that that particular colour contains.

thechakras

Chakras are the power centres through which primal energy – white light from the sun – is drawn into the body via our aura (*see p. 15*) to nourish and sustain our existence. Primal energy is the force necessary for all growth, and every living thing on the planet is dependent on it.

The seven major chakras are located at different points of the body, from the base of the spine to the top of the head, although their positions may vary slightly from person to person. In addition, many minor chakras exist – for example, in the fingertips, feet, shoulders, and hands. Chakras are not physical entities, but since they link the body and psyche they exert a powerful effect.

The word "chakra" comes from *chakrum*, the Sanskrit word for "wheel", which reflects the fact that chakras are constantly moving, continuously absorbing currents of energy. Each chakra is sensitive to a specific wavelength, or colour component, of what we call "white" light. The major chakras draw in the main colours of the rainbow (*see opposite*), which are absorbed and then circulated throughout the body. In a healthy person, the chakras take in and distribute this energy evenly – free-flowing energy is essential for health and wellbeing. If, however, an energy imbalance exists, it is likely that there is either too much or too little of a specific colour energy.

chakras and you

The need for different colours of light varies from person to person. Our mental, emotional, and physical health is based on the body obtaining a balanced flow of energy. Each chakra is influenced by the qualities of all the others. For example, a disfunctioning base chakra – affecting feelings of instinct, survival, and vitality – will influence the way in which the other centres function. When you are working to improve and balance the chakras, start with the base and work upward. The chakras are often compared to flowers opening and closing. The base chakra has four petals; the crown one thousand.

chakras in detail

RED: BASE CHAKRA Your physical strength and vitality are dependent on the correct and sufficient intake of this colour. A healthy red chakra reveals an energetic, passionate, confident, and well-grounded individual with positive energies. Other characteristics include a strong will and a person who is ambitious, assertive, pioneering, and persistent in life. Positive red feelings are expressed through warmth, friendship, excitement, and passion. Imbalance here leads to low physical activity and constant tiredness, and could indicate a lack of understanding of your own purpose, feelings of unworthiness, and explosive anger, resentment, and aggression. On the negative side, an imbalance of this colour could reflect a greedy, ruthless, and pushy nature.

ORANGE: SACRAL CHAKRA This centre covers the area of the digestive system and sexual organs. A healthy sacral chakra denotes an outgoing, sociable, party-loving person who is sporty, good-natured, and generous. It indicates an adventurous, spontaneous risk-taker, somebody able to communicate and interact well with others.

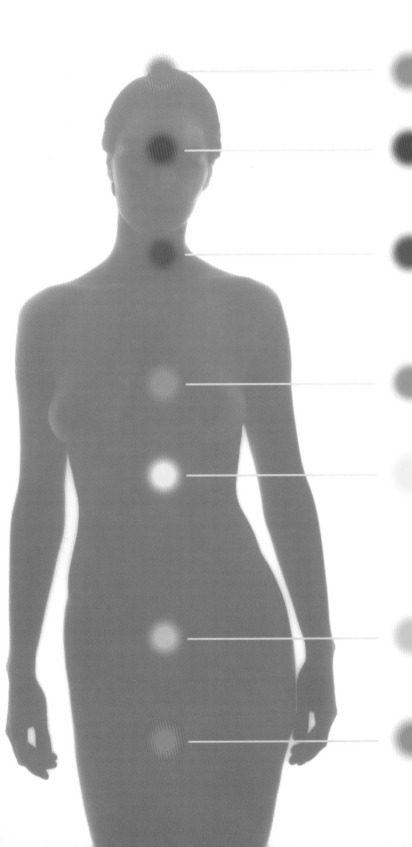

MAGENTA, WHITE, OR GOLD: CROWN CHAKRA
This is the centre of understanding, cognition, wisdom and knowledge, transcendence, and divinity. Governing organs/glands: cerebral cortex, central nervous system, and right eye.

VIOLET: BROW CHAKRA
This is the chakra of the third eye. It relates to insight, intuition, and clairvoyance. Governing organs/glands: pineal, pituitary, left eye, nose, ears, and spine.

BLUE: THROAT CHAKRA
This is the area of sound, vibration, and true communication connected to verbal and creative expression. Governing organs/glands: thyroid, parathyroid, hypothalamus, throat, and mouth.

GREEN: HEART CHAKRA
This is the area of love, balance, and self-acceptance. A balanced heart chakra radiates feelings of love, security, gentleness, and forgiveness. Governing organs/glands: heart, thymus, circulatory system, arms, hands, and lungs.

YELLOW: SOLAR PLEXUS CHAKRA
The centre of will, self-determination, intellect, ego, and personal power. When balanced, this reveals inner knowing, "gut feelings", and a sense of being in control. Governing organs/glands: pancreas, adrenals, stomach, liver, gall bladder, nervous system, and muscles.

ORANGE: SACRAL CHAKRA
The centre for sexuality and creativity. A healthy orange chakra indicates a sociable, outgoing nature in somebody enjoying good humour, fun, pleasure, and movement. Governing organs/glands: ovaries, testicles, prostate, genitals, spleen, womb, and bladder.

RED: BASE CHAKRA
Relates to instinct, survival, self-preservation, and your right to exist. A healthy base chakra implies vitality, grounding, and physical drive. Governing organs/glands: adrenals, kidneys, spinal column, colon, legs, and bones.

On the negative side are feelings of fear, unease, shyness, and timidity. This chakra relates to procreation, sexuality, physical force, and the proper assimilation of food. If it is not functioning properly, the digestive processes break down, leading to a loss of appetite, tiredness, and lack of vitality. A blockage here can lead to overindulgence in food or sex, sexual difficulties, and emotional problems.

YELLOW: SOLAR PLEXUS CHAKRA This centre vitalizes the nervous system, digestive processes, metabolism, and emotions. It is the centre of will, authority, self-control, and the intellect. It also influences self-determination and ego. When this chakra is healthy and balanced, it radiates a sense of being in control. Since yellow is connected to the intellect, it implies an inquisitive, analytical, discerning nature. Blockages here reveal feelings of powerlessness and disorientation, and a fear of loss. This fear can lead to a desire to control others – too much emphasis is placed on power and recognition, and anger and fear. When balanced, these areas of will and personal power reveal radiance, inner knowing, warmth, and light.

GREEN: HEART CHAKRA On the physical level, this centre is connected with the proper functioning of the heart, blood, and chest. An imbalance here involves problems such as high or low blood pressure and heart murmurs. A balanced heart chakra radiates feelings of security, of divine and unconditional love, and also of gentleness and forgiveness. It reveals an understanding and co-operative nature, and an appreciation for the simple things in life. This chakra not only governs the physical heart, but also the emotional problems and repressions that can result in heart attacks. Heart problems are often due to a fear of giving or a fear of involvement, or of being hurt. Negative expressions indicate a cautious, jealous, envious person, somebody who believes that life is unfair.

BLUE: THROAT CHAKRA The physical expression of this chakra is related to creative expression in speech, writing, and the arts. A healthy throat chakra denotes somebody who is able to know when and how to communicate in the best possible way. This implies integration, peace, truth and knowledge, honesty, and a kindly nature. Blockages in the area of this chakra can lead to communication and speech problems and also to feelings of withdrawal, the "blues", depression, apathy, inertia, detachment, and introversion.

VIOLET: BROW CHAKRA This chakra is located in the centre of, or just above, the eyebrows and it is often referred to as the "third eye". It relates to light, knowledge, and the mind. It influences your sensory organs of sight, sound, and smell, and it is the centre of intuition and reflection. When this chakra is operating well, you are capable of connecting with your spiritual, psychic, and clairvoyant abilities. This centre is also linked to your sense of self-respect. Blockages here lead to feelings of low self-worth and inferiority, and of feeling detached from the world. If this chakra becomes unbalanced you may develop a tendency to become abstract and dreamy.

MAGENTA, WHITE OR GOLD: CROWN CHAKRA This chakra vitalizes the upper brain (cerebrum), where finer spiritual forces enter your aura (see p. 15). The crown chakra is usually the last centre of all to open and it will continue to expand as you progress on your spiritual path. If this chakra shows any signs of imbalance, physical disorders may reveal themselves as headaches and migraines. Blockages may lead to confusion, a lack of inspiration, aloofness, depression, and alienation. When in balance this chakra shows itself as love and compassion. It reflects inner strength and a dignified, dedicated, and distinctive nature.

OUR AURA

We are all surrounded by an electromagnetic energy field known as an "aura" – a multilayered, pulsating energy of subtle emanations sometimes seen as a colour. Every body and every living thing has its own aura containing a record of life experiences – past and future. Whether the auric colours are seen as clear and bright or as muddy and murky reflects the state of your health. The colours change according to the thoughts and feelings coming from within, and what you experience from the world around you. A full range of spectral colours reflects a good state of health. Most of us can sense another person's aura, even if we are unable to see it. When meeting somebody for the first time, what we sense from that person's aura has a profound effect on us. White light is absorbed by our aura and is directed as various colour energies to the appropriate chakras. The aura and chakras are directly related to each other. A healthy aura means a healthy chakra system, and vice versa.

therainbow

Sunlight contains different frequencies of electromagnetic energy. When light passes through droplets of moisture in the air, each tiny envelope of water can become a prism, refracting the rays and causing each frequency to bend to a different degree. The result is a rainbow – one of nature's most dramatic displays.

Colour therapy utilizes the fact that each major colour of the rainbow is a different quality of light and that each vibrates at its own particular energy level.

colour associations

RED Having the slowest vibration, red is the most dense, heavy, and physical of all the colours. Red relates to instinct, survival, and physical drive. It is the colour of strength, vitality, sexuality, and passion. It increases body temperature and stimulates blood circulation. Too much red can lead to exhaustion.

ORANGE This is the colour of joy, movement, and dance. It is a great antidepressant and can help with repressed feelings and inhibitions. It encourages creativity, excitement, vibrancy, and humour. Too much orange, however, can result in irresponsibility.

YELLOW Being warm and optimistic, yellow is closely associated with sunlight. It is the colour of detachment and is related to control, will, and ego. It stimulates our intellect and logical mind, as well as helping with the digestive process. Too much can result in excessive mental stimulation, ego, detachment, and arguments.

GREEN This colour is balancing, harmonizing, and restful. Green is most closely associated with nature, of trusting in the process of life, of acceptance, compassion, caring, and sharing. Although green soothes the emotions and heals the heart, too much of this colour can result in indecision and static, inactive feelings.

TURQUOISE This is the colour to boost immunity. It not only builds up our physical immunity to protect us from colds and viruses, it also boosts our emotional immunity. It is a very cooling, youthful, expressive colour, and one that is good for relieving inflammatory conditions. Too much turquoise can lead to isolation and confusion.

BLUE This colour calms and comforts. It is restful, truthful, and peaceful. It is the colour of honesty, devotion, and aspiration. Blue slows things down, eases stress, tension, and pain. Too much blue, however, can become isolating, overly calming, and demotivating.

VIOLET This is the colour of introspection, meditation, contemplation, dignity, and respect, and it boosts self-esteem. It feeds the area of insight, intuition, and perception. It is a soothing and tranquil colour, but it is best avoided by those who tend to live too much in a fantasy world.

MAGENTA This gentle colour has the fastest vibration. It is the colour of letting go and moving on. It is the nurturing and protective colour of unconditional and spiritual love. Too much can lead to fanaticism and arrogance.

colourandlight

There are many ways to introduce more colour energy into your home. Stained-glass panels, for example, can replace plain-glass panes, or simply be suspended in front of a window to catch the light. Glass crystals can also be hung where air currents will cause them to twirl and throw off flashes of coloured brilliance.

Colour is a quality of light, and the source of all natural light is the sun – an awesome inferno constantly pouring energy into our atmosphere. We all need and respond to light. If natural sunlight is not present in sufficiently high quantities what can result is a potentially serious depressive illness known as Seasonal Affective Disorder (SAD), a condition that affects, at least to some degree, millions of people living in environments deprived of sunlight. The simplest way to experience the health-giving aspects of coloured light is to expose yourself to the sun. Natural daylight contains all the rainbow's hues, which is why it is such an important part of a healthy and healing home.

the power of colour

Colour therapists look deeply and sensitively into the healing vibrations of all the different colour energies, as well as into the individual requirements of their clients – and the results of therapy sometimes have life-changing consequences. Colour healing can actually work on the molecular cell structure of the body and, as a result, there is evidence of astounding success in treating different ailments. A typical treatment consists of exposing an individual to lights of different colours and intensities, as well as laying coloured silk over the body for a specific and monitored period of time.

Since exposure to coloured light has a more powerful therapeutic effect than exposure to coloured pigment can bring about, coloured light needs to be employed with great care, even when the light is being used in the home for purely decorative purposes. Green light, for example, is considered to be an unhealthy colour to have about the home – it is too static and plants will not thrive under it. Red light signals danger; it alerts your system and speeds up blood circulation. Soft orange light is joyful and pleasing and physically flattering. Yellow light can be uplifting in certain circumstances, if it is not overdone. Bear in mind that many artificial lights contain a yellow hue. Blue light is particularly calming and soothing, while violet light can have a tranquil effect.

Gold and silver colours are so inherently reflective that they add a very special illumination to any room. Silver is associated with change, movement, and knowledge; gold with high ideals, wisdom, and abundance. On a practical level, you can introduce these hues into your home with gold and silver leaf, metallic powders, paints, fabrics, and braiding.

Filtering light through a transparent medium is another way to bring the excitement of colour into your home. Light shining through glass crystal, for example, produces myriad sparkles, while glass chandeliers can also be used to great effect. Or you could use coloured glass bricks as large panels or room dividers. Simpler still, why not cover low-voltage light bulbs with a suitable coloured paint?

SPARKLE
Sparkle is a play of light – sunshine bouncing back from glass or metal, for example, or some bright light source flashing momentarily into view. Place glass or reflective objects strategically around a room so that they catch any incoming light and accentuate and multiply its glorious healing energy.

colour

andmood

energizing

Red is the colour of primal energy. It is the colour of passion and of strength, motivation, and physical drive. It rouses us to activity and fills us with the energy to get things done. It is the pioneering spirit, the revolutionary, the extrovert. Red is the colour of the base chakra and is associated with instinct, survival, and security. Red raises the blood pressure and quickens the heart beat. It increases body temperature, alerts, and excites.

vivid red

Red is the most dramatic colour in the spectrum. It is dense and powerful. The hot pinks and magenta used here alongside splashes of vivid red are strikingly different in character, and together they create a lively and fun-filled effect.

A little of these colours goes a long way. Of all the colour vibrations making up white light, red is the slowest, so too much red can become heavy and oppressive. Large amounts of red make a room look smaller, but in this room the clean white walls, ceiling, and floor help to retain a feeling of light and space. This blank canvas of white creates a clean backdrop that serves to accentuate the purity and clarity of these hot, fun colours.

This room certainly raises the pulse rate and it will soon dispel any feelings of sluggishness. These colours induce activity. The atmosphere is happy yet restless, and so can be a tonic for those low in energy or feeling lethargic or depressed. But balance is important – in time, the mixed messages of magenta and red and the lack of a complementary colour can become unsettling. Note how the green lines of the cushion and on the flower stems provide that essential balance. Magenta is quite opposite in character to red. It is a much finer, less physical, and more spiritual colour. It is the colour of the crown chakra; red is the colour of the base chakra. While red is dense and heavy, magenta is light and vibrant.

Near right The clean, white floor colour is the perfect foil for this combination of reds and pinks, allowing each hue to retain its clarity and fun.

Middle right The gold thread on the cushion adds another element to the room's colour theme. The difference in reflective qualities thrusts the metallic gold forward against a vibrant, glowing background of magenta and orange.

Opposite Painting one section of wall vivid red makes it a visual anchor point around which the many different tones and shades of red and pink can be added. If used on all the walls, the effect would have been overwhelming.

smoothclaret

Glowing smooth, red and rich, claret is a splendid colour. Using claret in sections, and by breaking it up with neutral creams and white, you prevent the intensity of this red from becoming oppressive. Instead, it creates bursts of strength, drive, power, and confidence.

Don't get carried away with red, as too much can lead to nervous tension, aggression, and anger. Red can induce overactivity, so use this colour carefully – in the right rooms and in the right quantities – to ensure it is an energizing force, not a depleting one. Just small sections of red can create dramatic results. People who wear a lot of red tend to be either bursting with energy and drive or feeling washed out.

Red is empowering. In a red meeting room, speakers tend to be fiery, forcefully sticking to their "agenda" and making their points. It is often used in bars to create a cosy, lively atmosphere that gets people talking to each other. The type of red, however, is important, especially in restaurants or dining rooms, as the aim is to encourage conversation and not heated argument. For this reason orange is sometimes more appropriate, since it creates a lighter atmosphere than claret red. Yellow and red are often used in fast-food outlets. They shout for attention, and children like them. But spending long periods under their influence is exhausting – effective, though, in getting customers quickly in and out.

Near right This rich, opulent claret red creates an intimate and inviting atmosphere. The light colours on the floor and furniture prevent the red on the walls from becoming overpowering.

Middle right Blocks of red, such as on this kitchen unit and sofa, can help to keep us on the go. The buff-coloured walls help to hold and contain these lively colours.

Opposite The red panel creates a dramatic focus in this room. In fact, it is so powerful that, given a choice of seating, most people would not want such strong colour energy directly on their back and would prefer to sit facing it rather than actually on it.

hotspice

Hot, spicy reds are vivid and intense and, being so concentrated, small quantities are enough to create powerful effects. Hot spice can be on the blue or orange side of red, and different variations thrown together result in an exotic mix of stunning colour depth.

Red is a primary colour veering either toward orange or violet. It is the hottest of all the colours and experiments show that red-painted walls actually increase the temperature of a room. Red warms the body, and so surrounding yourself with hot, spicy reds can even help to ward off a chill. Just as cool colours encourage rest and meditative relaxation, so hot colours promote activity. Red can speed up the pulse rate to such a degree that people with heart conditions should not wear red next to their chests, and they should also avoid large areas of red anywhere in their homes.

Red stimulates alertness – warning lights, fire extinguishers, and the like are red because they demand immediate attention. But too much hot red can become distracting and draining. The expression "seeing red" implies the force of this colour. Being the colour of the base chakra, red is connected to our baser instincts of survival (*see pp. 12–15*), and can help us to feel grounded and secure.

Like other warm colours, red appears to advance toward us, making rooms look smaller and more intimate. These spicy hues create a cosy and an inviting refuge.

Right The texture of the rich, velvet fabric deepens the intensity of this sensual, crimson red. The silver adds light and depth to create a sumptuous feeling, and the leopard print reinforces the primal nature of the colour.

Opposite These hot, spicy hues are very welcoming, and this setting would create an ideal entrance or reception area. However, in general they are best balanced by a decorative scheme that includes some of the cooler colours.

exotic heat

Opulent eastern fabrics are often layered to create a feast of vibrant, glowing, exotic colour and heat. Gold and silver threads are interwoven with these colours in order to heighten their majestic qualities, and create a brilliant, luxurious, and alluring room.

The sheer translucency of the Indian sari fabrics used as window curtains in the picture shown opposite filter the daylight in subtle shades of red and orange as it enters the room. Hung in layers like this, the filtering effect of the material is intensified so that the result is an intimate red glow that seems to radiate its presence throughout the room. And the purity of the colours

Right Layer sheer fabrics together to produce an atmosphere of luxuriant decadence. Brilliant gold and silver cushions add their own special elevating touch to most colour schemes, but perhaps just one may be enough.

Opposite Mixing various fabrics and patterns together has created a lively and vibrant feeling in this comfortable-looking corner, and the enveloping shape of the space seems cosy and inviting.

in the silk fabric transmits a clean, clear, and nourishing quality of light much valued by colour healers.

Other characteristics of the sari fabric also make their own contribution to the overall effect on the light. Note how the tiny sequins in the fabric catch the light, thereby adding sparkle, movement, and energy to the room. Glass beads also catch the sunlight and act as if they are miniature prisms, refracting the light before sending it across the room. And the gold and silver threads and embroidery enhance the magic and thrill of these altogether exotic colours.

Gold is considered a male colour of abundance, wisdom, and high ideals. Silver is considered a female colour of movement, change, and knowledge. Gold is often easier to employ alongside hot colours, such as these reds and oranges, and silver is usually a better choice to associate with cooler colours, such as blue and violet.

The reds, oranges, and yellows of this room harmonize well and sit alongside each other on the colour wheel (*see pp. 8–9*). As an overall scheme, however, splashes of opposite and complementary colours help to impart more of a sense of balance. The opposite colour to red is turquoise, the opposite to orange is blue. If you are unsure which is the right shade of complementary colour to use, stare at a patch of the colour you want to harmonize it with in natural daylight for some seconds and then immediately look straight at a white wall to see an image of the appropriate complementary colour.

firedearth

The rich, earthy tones of the red used in the bathroom opposite bring to mind the colour and mood of an earlier era, a time before chemical dyes were introduced. Rather than appearing dull and muddy, red is rich, strong, and grounding.

Although cultures assign different values and associations to specific colours, for many red is a symbol of the life-force and, when used with gold, denotes the glory and majesty of physical life.

Because rich reds can become draining, they can be very effective in smaller rooms in which we spend only short periods of time. But red also brings life and interest, especially in rooms that receive little natural light. In a hallway, for example, where coats are hung up, red can be very welcoming. Just a quick and fleeting exposure to red can be enough to give your drive and energy levels a special boost. Painting the insides of cabinets in red, perhaps in the kitchen, for example, exposes you to short bursts of energetic red every time you open a cabinet door. Passageways and entrance halls are suitable areas for a burst of red energy. In workplaces, red in corridors encourages people to pass through quickly and get where they are going without stopping to chat to other people. In children's playrooms, small splashes of red, if combined with other colours, can be stimulating without being overexciting. It is often best to avoid having red in rooms used for relaxing, working, studying, and sleeping.

Left In small rooms, such as a bathroom, where you don't tend to linger for overlong periods, red supplies a boost of powerful energy without leaving you feeling drained or washed out.

Opposite These Chinese lanterns, with their golden yellow detailing, exemplify the life, excitement, and power of red. Coloured paper lanterns are a simple, charming, and inexpensive method of bringing coloured light into your home.

uplifting

Orange and yellow are uplifting colours, stimulating and enlivening. Orange, being the colour of the sacral chakra, is the hue most closely associated with joy and excitement, movement, and creativity. Yellow, at the solar plexus chakra, is connected to the ego, will, intellect, and feelings of detachment. Although orange and yellow radiate distinctly different energies, both are warm and optimistic colours with the ability to cheer our mood and raise our spirits.

orangeglow

Deep orange glows like a flame – warming, enchanting, and captivating. Orange is the colour that draws us into the excitement and fun of a vibrant, delightful energy that is full of movement, dance, and celebration.

Orange is formed by mixing red and yellow, and carries with it the heat and drive of red, albeit in a less-intense form, with elements of the lighter, more thoughtful and intellectual nature of yellow.

Orange is a sociable, party-loving colour that relates to creativity, excitement, fun, and humour. In the home, it creates an atmosphere conducive to movement and action and supplies the energy to achieve, create, express, and explore. This exciting, outgoing colour can lift you right out of the doldrums. It is a great antidepressant.

As orange is the colour of the sacral chakra, which partly governs the area of the digestive system, it is a good colour for kitchens or dining rooms. It can stimulate the appetite and can be especially helpful for people who undereat. Orange aids not only our physical digestion, it can also help us to digest life with joy, to accept matters, and to sort them out.

In both the rooms here, a radiant orange is supported and contained by soft gray tones. The neutrality of gray helps to accentuate the vibrancy of the orange glow.

Right Since vivid orange can be too powerful when used as an overall colour, it is best to introduce it, as here, in small sections only. Used like this, you can achieve a brilliant and fiery impact, yet one that is not overwhelming.

Opposite This brightly coloured kitchen is an exciting and stimulating room in which to meet, eat, and discuss. The cool stainless-steel and gray worktops help to balance the vivacity of the cabinet and drawer fronts.

burntorange

Like many of the autumnal hues, burnt orange contains just hints of red-brown. So rather than becoming murky, it is transformed into a rich, intense, earthy colour. As bright orange is very powerful, this toned-down version can be far easier to integrate into your home.

To avoid the problem of orange being too potent an influence, many people confine its use in the home to colour accents only. The wooden screen in the room opposite is a perfect example of this. You can also make a paper screen in varying degrees of colour strength and translucency. Once fixed to a wooden frame, all you need do is position it to catch and filter any sunlight entering the room from behind. The pale blue panels of this screen add an essential element of balance to the orange tones of the room. Blue is the opposite and complementary colour to orange, and contains all its opposite characteristics. So, in this way, a harmonious and balanced atmosphere is achieved.

Orange is the outgoing, exuberant colour of movement and creativity, while blue is the calm and quiet of introspection. Blue, like orange, is connected to creativity. Orange is linked to the physical side and blue more to the literate aspects of the arts and imagination. Blue and orange sharpen each other, bringing out each other's opposite natures. Used in equal quantities they can cause conflict, but in the small panels of this screen they simply balance one another.

You can also use paper directly over a window, changing the colour to suit your mood. When mixing various tones, try to keep the colour as pure as possible. A dull orange will not reflect the glory of this high-spirited and effervescent energy.

Left This coloured
lampshade produces a
pure and gentle orange
light, which adds a simple
yet inviting glow to the
room. This, together with
the soft peach colours
contained in the screen,
creates a radiant form
of orange energy.

Opposite The burnt
orange accents of this
vase, its flowers, and
the cup and saucer
combine to provide a
truly resplendent orange
energy. You can use
small "tester" pots of
paint on objects, such as
vases, boxes, and picture
frames, since just the
slightest quantity of paint
is all that is needed to
transform them.

orange**zest**

Orange is the colour of enthusiasm and gusto, of delight, and of a zest for life. It is often felt to be the most sociable of all the colours. It gets people up on their feet, talking and dancing, and having fun. This makes it an ideal colour for entertaining and dining areas.

Right Orange and red are the most stimulating and active of all the colours. When they are teamed together, as seen here in this table and chairs, the result is inevitably a lively and an exciting one making an ideal environment for spirited and playful meetings.

Below right The pale blue splashback at the window in the background brings a cool balance to the hot and lively colours of this dining area.

Opposite Since blue is the complementary to orange, the blues in the background of the butterfly wall picture act to counter and moderate the influences of the orange tones that are used in this part of the room. The gray of the table base, wastebin, and chairs help to corral and define the otherwise very lively colour scheme.

In common with the other warm colours, orange appears visually to advance and so tends to close down space, making rooms appear cosy and intimate. It is a suitable colour for many rooms in the home with the exception, usually, of bedrooms or the study. These are both retreat areas in the home in which the stimulating qualities of orange may be inappropriate.

Orange is not the ideal colour to use if you are feeling stressed or you are too easily agitated. And if you or members of your family tend to be naturally very outgoing and flamboyant, perhaps consider using more calming colours, since the presence of too much orange can lead to fickle and irresponsible behaviour.

summer**sun**

The gentle, radiant yellow of the glowing summer sun is an expansive and optimistic colour, one that is light, pure, positive, and uplifting in nature. Like sunshine itself, the enchanting shades of yellow can be especially appreciated when seen first thing in the morning.

Despite the cheerful qualities of yellows, it is wise to use them carefully in the home as they carry with them complex and sometimes difficult issues. Yellow is a primary pigment colour, between orange and green on the colour wheel (*see pp. 8–9*). It is the colour of the third chakra, positioned at the solar plexus, and carries many emotional issues of ego, control, and will. Yellow is also much associated with mental energy and activity – the left side of the brain. It is connected to matters of the intellect and detachment, and induces a rational, discerning approach linked to mental control. Too much yellow, therefore, can encourage excessive thought and ego, but if used in the right areas, and balanced with cooler, more contained colours, these vast, boundless yellows can create a resounding and glorious support. Like the summer sun, these colours can be welcoming, warming, and gracious.

Right Orange and yellow together create a lively and very stimulating decor, but it is one that needs to be balanced with cooler, more restrained colours. The cool green tint of the glass partition in this room helps to create a sense of colour balance.

Opposite The deep blue of the refrigerator adds a strong sense of balance to this essentially yellow kitchen – the strength of the blue seems to anchor the expansive nature of this colour. The clear-glass brick wall partition is a simple yet effective device for maximizing every scrap of daylight in this small, enclosed area.

sunshine

Golden yellow is the colour closest to sunshine. These radiant hues light up any part of your home to create a wonderfully lustrous, burnished glow. However, these expansive hues are often best balanced with an equally strong cool colour to hold them in check.

Yellow is often a popular colour choice for those of a more analytical or intellectual bent, as it tends to have a stimulating effect on these mental qualities. It is, however, not generally recommended for social rooms, since if the ego becomes too assertive (*see p. 42*), heated debate and argument can result. It is also not recommended in bedrooms, where mental stimulation makes sleeping none too easy. And be warned, if you decide to opt for a predominantly yellow living room, you may find that you end up doing rather more reading than socializing.

Yellow can be perfect in a study or games room, where an increase in mental activity will help to keep you sharp and alert. The sunshine colour of the chairs opposite will stimulate mental activity, making this perhaps better as an area to discuss work rather than general socializing.

Right The strong blue of the vase in this group creates a perfect complementary balance to the yellow and orange hues. Position coloured glass carefully so that its colour is illuminated by transmitted light.

Far right In a dull corridor without much natural daylight, this pure yellow door adds a sense of brightness and direction. It can be particularly appropriate as the colour for the door to a study or home office (*see above*).

Opposite The slate gray surface of the table top and the collection of water-worn pebbles add a feeling of weight and grounding to the decorative scheme of this room. This helps to support the light and airy expanse of white wall and yellow fabric.

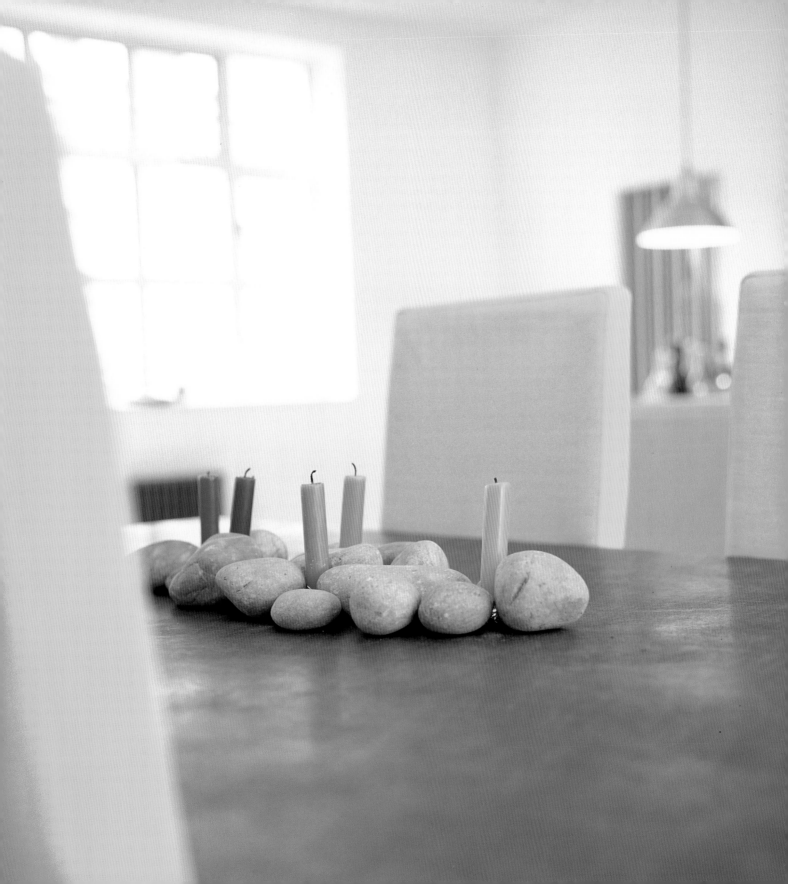

sunflower

The vivid brightness of sunflowers basking in the midday sun makes a strong, pure, bold, and powerful colour image. When used with discretion around the home, this mighty yellow produces a fearless decorative statement – one that is unwavering in its impact.

This is most definitely a wake-up colour, and in this kitchen and bathroom such an intense burst of sunflower yellow can prove helpful for those who take too much time coming to every morning and who need to be snapped quickly out of sleep mode. And since the kitchen opposite is painted in such a mentally stimulating colour, this may easily become the preferred area for informal study or children's homework.

Violet is the opposite and complementary colour to yellow. While yellow is the colour of the intellect, violet is connected more to intuition; when these colours are used together, you have balance. The gray areas of the stainless steel in the kitchen and bathroom perform a containing role on the yellow, but note how, in particular, the blue tint to the light above the cooker creates that crucial element of balance.

Right With the beautiful surface characteristics of satin as a base, the sunflower yellow of this fabric literally glows, while the beaded edging catches the sun to create yet more light and sparkle.

Far right Under the influence of the strong yellow in this bathroom, you may feel like reading a book or newspaper. So bold a yellow is mentally very stimulating and will certainly get your thoughts racing.

Opposite Using yellow as strong and powerful as this in a kitchen is not a good idea for a couple with a shaky relationship. The colour energy here can create feelings of ego, one-upmanship, argument, and conflict.

fruitpastels

Some fruity shades of orange and yellow combine to create a sweet and luscious flavour all of their own. The soft, creamy yellow in this kitchen, for example, is smooth like butter, tender, mild, and reassuring – altogether a softer, lighter impact of pale yellow.

Painting a gentle pastel or, indeed, a clear, more vibrant colour over dark and heavy hues has an immediate transforming effect. And with the many special paint primers currently on the market, this type of radical colour make-over is readily achieved. Most rooms can be repainted and given a new lease of life. But don't ignore the details, either – even changing knobs and handles can create an entirely new style and character.

Since the kitchen is generally the most expensive room in the home to change, a transformation here using paint and colour can be simple and cost-effective. Even floors can be painted, using special paints and varnishes, and colours can be specified as accurately as your imagination allows. Most surfaces – even ceramic tiles and splashbacks – can now be primed and painted.

Once you include crockery, packaging, and the many other decorated items found in kitchens, this room is probably also the most colourful room in the home, and paint can be used to impose coherence and harmony. You can choose items for painting as a means to satisfy temporary colour attractions. Painting

small pieces of furniture, such as the orange drawers below, can serve this purpose. A strong attraction to orange, for example, can be connected to creative energy and your need for a lighter, more fun and joyful approach to life.

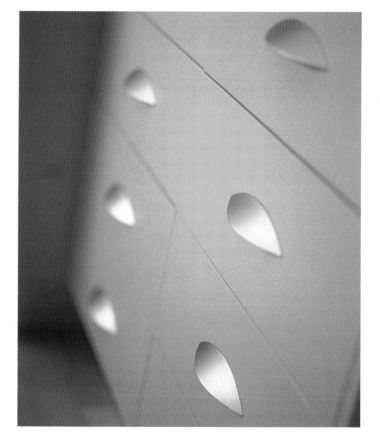

Right When revamping furniture to give it a smooth, glass-like colour finish, try using a spray gun to apply the paint. Even laminated finishes can be effectively primed and then painted this way.

Opposite The charming and gentle blue of this kitchen table creates a cooling balance to the surrounding yellow hues. The blue/gray larder doors add a sense of structure and support to these essentially light and airy colours.

balancing

Green is the colour associated with balance and harmony. It is in the middle of the visible spectrum and it is the neutral colour – neither hot nor cold. Green represents equilibrium. It is the colour of the heart chakra and is healing for all matters concerning the heart. Green is also the colour of nature. It is honest, stable, and reliable. It is the colour of kindness, compassion, caring, and sharing. Green is comforting and stress-relieving.

limetwist

Green is a secondary colour formed by mixing blue and yellow pigments. Lime hues contain more yellow than blue, making them active, alert, and lively. The softer, leafy tones of lime are fresh and spring-like, reflecting the vibrant qualities of fertility and growth.

Green is created by mixing cool and warm colours. This unique balance means green is the only colour the eye needs no adjustment to see. Limes are slightly more active than other shades of green, but too much yellow in lime, like yellows that are on the green side, feels challenging and unsettling, even nauseous, to many people.

Symbolically, green is associated with a circle – balanced, harmonious, and complete. The round table in the breakfast room opposite enhances the qualities of the green walls, making a perfect area for group discussions. Green

is an ideal colour for rooms in which difficult decisions have to be made, as its balancing and supportive nature is not conducive to argument or conflict.

The green colour range is most associated with nature and the countryside, reminding us of the healing that comes through the natural world. Green is calming and soothing, connecting us to the unconditional and constant support we receive from nature. When life is difficult and stressful, the greens of the grass, plants, and trees are always there to help and soothe us.

Near right A colourful glass-bead room-divider adds a sparkling touch of light and movement to this green-coloured kitchen. As in nature, green combines well with an array of vibrant colours.

Middle right We all respond to colour in a personal way. Some will find the lime of this kitchen balancing and peaceful; others may find it sharp and unsettling.

Opposite These vibrant lime green chairs blend naturally with the emerald green walls. Blocks of white, colourful flowers, and plenty of natural daylight combine to balance the overall effect and keep the room feeling bright and lively.

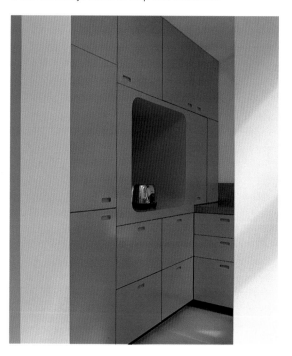

emeraldflair

This powerful emerald green is the colour of the rich, pure-green light that you can see in a rainbow. Since it is such an intense form of green, it carries with it a lot of colour energy, and so it is generally best used in sections, broken up and lightened with white.

An important factor in creating a balanced colour scheme is the introduction of opposite, or complementary, colour. In nature, colour balance often happens naturally – red or magenta flowers, berries, and fruit against green foliage. Nature always provides perfect colour inspirations.

Green is the colour associated with the fourth chakra, located in the heart area, and so is connected to matters of the heart. On the physical level, this includes the functioning of the organs close to the heart region, such as the lungs, the chest, and the whole circulatory system.

It can be helpful for somebody suffering from asthma or bronchitis. Green also helps to balance the flow of blood, and it is interesting that doctors and nurses often wear green gowns in the operating theatre. On an emotional level, green can help with matters relating to the heart. It can soothe our apprehensions of giving and our fear of being hurt. This is not only connected to romantic love but also to the type of love that teaches us to accept people for what they are – not what we might prefer them to be. Green is gentle, forgiving, and nurturing and can help calm the distress of a broken heart.

Near right Satin finishes on kitchen cabinet doors intensify the effect of strong colours. Shiny gloss finishes reflect more light and create more depth of glowing colour.

Middle right These two opposite colours, green and magenta, enhance and enrich one another, producing a magical contrast. As a result, the magenta flowers appear more magenta; the green walls more green.

Opposite The vibrant red of these cherries creates a wonderfully vivid decorative contrast to the rich emerald green of the walls. The tiniest splash of red against this green immediately catches the eye.

spea**rmint**

Spearmint is a shade of green that contains more blue pigment than yellow. It is a watery, restful colour, one that generates more of the qualities associated with turquoise and blue to create a calming, cooling, and refreshing atmosphere.

Right Because of the strong blue influence in the green used here, these closet doors take on more the qualities of turquoise, producing a clear, lively, and refreshing effect. This results in a nourishing expanse of colour that almost appears to glow with energy.

Opposite The lively pink colour-washed effect used on the door and radiator cover creates an effective balance of complementary colour when set against these minty green walls. The cool and gentle green wall colour contains the excitement of the multicoloured bedspread.

As is often expressed so perfectly in nature, shades of spearmint green, like many others in this colour range, are best used in broken, mottled, or variegated fashion. Some broken paint effects are perfect for adding life and light to a wall finish. A white or an off-white basecoat, for example, can help to bring out movement and vitality from underneath a transparent wash of green-coloured glaze. But it is important to retain a sense of balance by not using too much green in a room – especially solid, unbroken green – as this can create a feeling of stagnancy leading, in turn, to indifference and inertia. Too much green, like too much of any colour, can lead to an imbalance of energy and detrimental consequences. Green is also associated with envy – "green with envy" and "green-eyed monster" are both terms used when the heart is not balanced.

Greens are suitable for relaxation areas, such as the rooms here. Because of its general healing qualities, green is said to be the most beneficial colour. And being a restful colour, it is often chosen for hospitals. In theatres, actors relax in the "green room" before going on stage. Green can also be excellent in a study and for decision-making areas, such as an office meeting room or boardroom. It would be an ideal choice for a law court, creating an impartial, harmonious atmosphere. But it should be avoided in areas where a lot of activity is crucial.

meadowgreen

Because of their obvious associations with nature, greens in general, and the meadow shades of green in particular, can be very comforting and easy to live with – especially so for people living and working in urban areas with little access to parks or the countryside.

Balance is achieved not only through the use of colour, but also as a result of the lines, shapes, and patterning contained within a room. The gentle curves of the round-backed sofa echoing the shape of the curved partition in the living room opposite, for example, create a satisfying sense of balance by countering the hard and angular lines of the walls. The circular shape seen in the wall painting and the round-faced clock above the fireplace both help to reinforce this sense of balance.

Many modern buildings have regular, geometrically-shaped spaces and rooms, and in such areas the soft lines in furniture and furnishings can exert a powerful moderating and balancing influence. Large plants, like the one below, can also help to soften hard lines. Any pattern in the room based on natural themes and motifs will also be supportive of this. Green is often a good colour choice near windows that overlook grass, trees, or plants, as it serves to introduce the greens of nature into your home.

Right The open-plan arrangement and unusual structure of this living area give rise to exciting opportunities for creative paint effects. The high placement of these blocks of gentle colour creates a surprising and interesting feature, one that echoes, supports, and balances the colours below.

Opposite This gentle shade of green is peaceful and calming, creating an atmosphere that positively invites you to sit down, relax, and pick up the book.

greentouches

Every room and practically every colour scheme would benefit from the addition of the natural greens of the plant world. There are plants of every conceivable green to provide you with just the right colour accents for balance and harmony.

Right This apple green and violet paint combination creates a vivid colour theme, while the mirrored doors multiply the amount of light available in the room. This is especially effective on protruding walls that break up the symmetry of a room as the mirrors reflect a feeling of space where it is missing.

Green is the perfect colour for creating a sense of calm and balance. Ideally, however, all decoration should in its own way create a harmonious and balanced environment. When choosing colours for a specific room, think about both the cool and the warm sides of the colour wheel (*see pp. 8–9*). Three main colours used in varying proportions can form the basis of a balanced colour scheme. Even though there are varieties of green that work well with every other colour, green is sometimes best confined to an accent only, since in excess it can become too still and static. Green touches, however, are gladly received in every room. Just as green plants and flowers are welcome everywhere in the home, so splashes of green can prove to be the next best thing. Painting furniture, such as the wardrobe opposite, is an easy way to introduce a pleasing touch of green.

As important as colour is for balance, don't ignore other factors, such as shape, texture, and lighting. Placing objects in pairs can be balancing and comforting. In feng shui, room features and furniture are carefully positioned to create a balanced and healthy flow of energy.

Left It can be rewarding to get away from the more predictable approaches to colour usage in the home. In this stylish kitchen, the ceiling has been painted in a colour that closely matches that of the chair. Not only does this approach help to establish a firm sense of balance in the room, it is also a fun effect.

refreshing

Turquoise is a mixture of green and blue, and it has something of the nature of both. It is vibrant and youthful in character, reviving and invigorating. Like the colours of pure, fresh water, turquoise is cool and clean, with a clarity that can ease the flow of communication and expression. Turquoise is protective, boosting both our physical and our emotional immunity. It soothes away tension and stress, and can help whenever we feel vulnerable and nervous.

clearturquoise

The clarity and strength of this clear turquoise makes it a stunning, vibrant hue, one that is full of impact and influence. Like the semiprecious turquoise stone, this deep and opulent colour carries with it an abundance of vivid colour energy.

It sometimes helps to understand a colour by comparing it with its opposite – in this case, strong, clear red, the hot colour of physical drive and passion. Turquoise complements these qualities, bringing peace, rest, and calm. Red spurs us to get up and go; turquoise calls us back to relax. As red advances, making rooms appear smaller, so turquoise recedes to make rooms seem larger and more spacious. With its mighty youthful nature, a strong, clear turquoise can encourage clarity, openness, and change. If, however, you are feeling rather on the slow and sluggish side, then turquoise is not necessarily the most

helpful colour and you should perhaps be looking for something more stimulating, such as orange.

The walls of this living room have been gently mottled. This is an ideal way to apply such a vivid colour, since its intensity remains despite the fact that the overall effect is lighter and more gentle. Like blue, turquoise is best avoided in cold rooms. This essentially turquoise space is perfect for relaxing in or cooling down, although it could be too detached for socializing and entertaining without the presence of the warmer colours.

Near right The red in this cushion creates a vibrant balance when seen against the turquoise of the chair, whose velvet fabric intensifies the depth of this jewel-like hue.

Middle right Trying out paints and different techniques is an ideal means of exploring new hues and effects. The supporting surface could be any piece of light board, a strip of primed lining paper, or even a masked-off area of wall.

Opposite The wall mirrors in this room, together with the white ceiling, add to the expansive feeling of the turquoise. The pink of the cushions and the peachy colour in the paintings give an essential touch of gentle warmth.

coolwaters

The turquoise part of the spectrum is cleansing, uplifting, and vibrant. The clarity of this colour makes it bubbly, alert, and spirited, conveying feelings of vivacious freshness. Like the cool of a mountain stream, turquoise helps to soothe away tension and stress.

Right By combining various shades of turquoise and blue pigments yourself, you can create subtle shifts in colour balance for application on walls or pieces of furniture. Add touches of extra blue, green, or white to create a highly personalized colour scheme for your home.

Opposite Like many blue-coloured kitchens, the use of turquoise produces a cooling, calming, and peaceful working arena in what, after all, can be the hottest, most hectic room in the home. The particular shade of turquoise used in this kitchen is especially clear and vibrant.

Turquoise contains something of the qualities of the two colours from which it is derived – the soothing, peace-making aspects of blue, and the balance of green, which is the colour of the heart chakra. Turquoise is for protection and immunity, helping to ward off colds and hay fever, while its cooling qualities can settle inflammatory and swelling conditions. It is used to treat cuts, burns, and skin problems such as eczema.

Cool turquoise not only protects the physical body from germs and viruses, it also shields you mentally and emotionally. If you feel that others are taking too much of a toll on the inner you, then turquoise energy could be what you need. If you are feeling nervous or vulnerable, let turquoise calm and comfort you like the cool waters of a beautiful lake.

The cool vibrancy of this kitchen colour makes it ideal for use in hot climates. The dark brown wooden floor is very grounding but this room would benefit from more colour to add a lively warmth and balance. When seen in action, however, with the worktops full of colourful fruits, vegetables, and packages, this kitchen takes on a harmonious appearance.

aquamarine

Aquamarine is the fresh and watery colour of the clear and exotic Caribbean or Mediterranean sea. And just like the uplifting effect that being by the sea has on us, so these colours are the embodiment of coolness, vitality, and soothing relaxation.

Right The green and pale blue floor colour adds to the gentle watery theme of this bedroom. Painting or colour-washing floorboards is a simple yet effective way of adding subtle colour to a room. After painting, you can seal the boards with a protective floor wax or varnish.

Opposite Lying in a bath staring upward as you relax can take on a whole new meaning if you paint the ceiling in one of your favourite colours. The aquamarine in this bathroom is extremely soothing, while the warm tones of the floor and bath surround provide essential colour balance and harmony.

The blues and greens of nature are often mottled and variegated in appearance. In a decorative scheme, mottled paint finishes can be effective in softening colour, creating light, and introducing movement. Think of your home as a canvas, blank surfaces on which you can express yourself through not only colour, but also pattern and shape, both of which exert their own influence and energy.

In the bedroom here, an abstract pattern has been washed on to the wall. The broken paint effect is watery and restful, and turns a plain wall into an interesting feature. A thin solution of paint was washed on to a basecoat of a lighter colour – in this case, white or off-white. While the rectangular sections here are gentle and abstract, a harder, more regulated pattern can have an opposite effect. Bold, striped patterns, for example, can be discordant and disturbing, and strong geometric pattern can result in restless, disturbed sleep. Patterns in contrasting colours can be eye-catching but they quickly become taxing, and large, formal patterns can be dominating and unnerving in a bedroom. These patterns would be better in hallways – transitory spaces in which you don't spend a lot of time.

The use of coloured and frosted glass in the bathroom illustrated opposite is an exciting way to see transparency and colour. Glass bricks and panels can be installed to create partitions that ensure privacy without subtracting the light. This frosted turquoise glass has been magically illuminated by the ceiling light behind it.

azurespa

Receding and expansive like the blue of the skies, the charm of azure lies in its lightness and airiness. Azure is an ideal colour for opening up confined spaces and less-spacious rooms, such as small bathrooms and shower rooms, which can feel claustrophobic.

Right Showering in this expanse of brilliant turquoise would make a refreshing start to any day. And with your naked skin absorbing this strong and vibrant colour, your body's immune system is likely to receive a boost, too.

Opposite The sky blue ceiling in this bathroom adds to the feeling of space and relaxation created by the turquoise-coloured walls. This pastel tint is less powerful than the stronger turquoise of the shower room and so its impact will be correspondingly lessened.

With its restorative qualities, turquoise is an ideal colour to accompany your shower or bath, especially after exercising or at the end of a hot day. You will often find turquoise used on packaging for sport-related shower gels and deodorants. It is a colour to enjoy most when you feel like a boost of freshness and cool protection.

Turquoise is especially linked to the body's immunity. It is the colour of the little-recognized thymus chakra, which is positioned between the throat and heart chakras (see pp. 12–15). The thymus works with the immune system, producing the antibodies that protect us from disease. Turquoise is also connected to the flow of speech and can help us with social interaction by enhancing our ability to communicate effectively.

These cool azure shades of turquoise are particularly suitable for bathrooms as they are a reminder of natural, fresh, and cleansing water. Since we absorb colour most easily through naked skin, the bath- or shower room is an ideal place to be exposed to extra colour. Azure is often teamed with blue, especially in hot climates, and is a colour best used in its purest form, lightened only with white.

glacier**blue**

Being principally blue in colour, but containing just a touch of green, these glacier-like hues are cool, fresh, icy, and, above all, still and calming. They are ideal for those of us with hot, firey tempers, where their soothing qualities can really be made to tell.

Right It is interesting to note the impact the red towel has in the foreground of this ice-cool turquoise bathroom. The blue and orange feature tiles on the basin splashback are opposite and contrasting hues, and when they are presented like this in equal quantities they seem to vie strongly with each other for your attention.

Opposite The bright white bed linen in this bedroom serves to reinforce the icy cool clarity of the walls. This is definitely a soothing bedroom for the seriously stressed and overheated.

A bedroom painted in these colours can be perfect for those with stressful, mentally demanding jobs, especially if you find it difficult to switch off, let go, and breathe out at the end of the day. Glacier blues are soothing and stress relieving. These cool versions of blue are ideal for use in particularly hot rooms; if, however, you are thinking of using them in rooms that receive little natural daylight, then you may find that these glacier colours are simply too chilling to feel comfortable in winter. Bearing in mind the importance of colour balance, you need to consider introducing splashes of red somewhere within the room. In these examples, you can see how the orange tones of the bathroom furniture and the wooden flooring in the bedroom sit so well with the cool and calming colour of the walls. The addition of the warmth of the orange helps to create a cosy, inviting environment.

An attraction to the purity of these clean hues is a healthy sign in itself, while a preference for more muddy tones could reflect a confusion and insecurity associated with those colours. The coolness of the glacier blues helps to calm the mind and encourage clarity of thought.

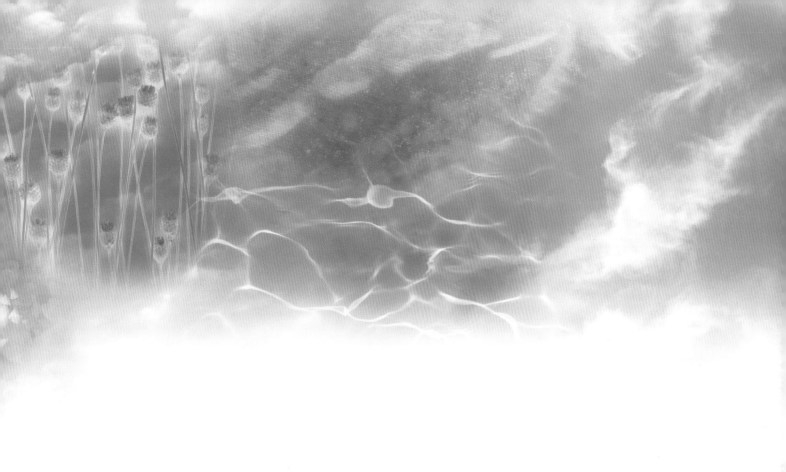

calming

Blue is the colour for calm. Like a clear summer's sky, it is infinite and heavenly. Blue is cooling, pacifying, and comforting and it helps us to wind down, adopt a more leisurely pace, and simply relax. It slows the heartbeat, blood pressure drops, and we begin to breathe more deeply as blue relaxes both the muscles and the mind. Blue is the colour for communication, imagination, and inner strength. With it comes quiet, peace, and serenity.

deepblue

Deep blue is the rich and distant hue of the bluest Mediterranean sky. This colour's strength of character carries great impact, containing as it does a wealth of deep blue energy. It is intense and powerful, creating a restful, peaceful sense of calm.

Right The light, warm tones of this wooden floor, together with the clean, white skirting board, lift and balance the intensity of the richly coloured walls. Two strong blues used together like this make a bold statement and have a calming impact.

Opposite Subtle orange skin tones in the picture above the bed stand out against the deep blue of the walls. Orange is the complementary colour to blue and adds a gentle touch of warmth and balance. The bright white wall and bed linen reflect all the available light in the room, and so bring clarity to the wall colour.

Blue is a primary colour and cannot be formed by combining other colours. On the colour wheel, blue sits between violet and green and can take on the tendencies of both these colours; however, the deep blues depicted in these rooms have neither violet nor green undertones. In terms of decorating, you will find more varieties of blue than of any other colour. Blue is firmly on the cool side of the wheel and, in common with all cool colours, appears to recede from the viewer to produce a sense of space.

In the home setting, deep blue is very effective when contrasted with white to reflect as much light as possible around the room. In Mediterranean countries, whitewashed buildings reflect light and heat to keep interiors cool, and buildings look whiter than white against the sky. The white of the clouds against the blue of the sky is purifying and uplifting.

Good, restful sleep is almost guaranteed in bedrooms painted in a dark-blue colour scheme. This colour encourages a more peaceful night and is especially helpful for those who habitually take their work home and find it difficult to switch off and relax. It also discourages

nightmares and promotes better dreams. It is not, however, a colour to help get you out of bed in the morning. The version of blue shown here is particularly deep and definitely not for the sluggish, who may need a kick-start to the day.

electric blue

Electric blue is clear, clean, and bright and gleams with jewel-like intensity. It is extremely effective when used in small areas, such as alcoves and cabinets. Whether it has a satin finish or a polished sheen, this colour radiates a gentle glow.

In many traditions, blues are used in kitchen and crockery decoration, and as a cooling colour for food cupboards. In a working kitchen it encourages you to take your time over preparing the food, but for a kitchen-diner it may make people withdraw into themselves. Being such a cool colour, electric blue is not for rooms that receive little direct sunlight. Splashes of orange or yellow will introduce contrast and balancing warmth.

If colours become too sharp and electric, they can trigger nervous reactions. Very bright blues can become almost fluorescent in nature, thereby losing their gentle, calming qualities – however, the blue and turquoise used in this kitchen are simply vibrant, rich, and glowing in effect.

Blue is helpful for overactive conditions as it is such a calming colour. It reduces blood pressure and slows the heart. Its cooling influence is healing for burns and sunburn, and it eases tension headaches and general stress. Absorbing blue can be used to treat asthmatic conditions and it can be particularly helpful for premenstrual tension and pain. Blue is the best colour for easing pain of any sort.

Near right This unit has been painted in an array of vibrant blocks of colour, creating a near-abstract design. The blue bay appears even more striking with its complementary, orange, in view.

Middle right Stainless-steel worktops and surfaces harmonize well with this cool blue. The reflective surfaces act like mirrors, bouncing light back and forth to generate life and energy.

Opposite The golden colouring of the table brings balance to the blue colour scheme, but notice how the red wall switch jumps out and demands your attention. The eye is naturally drawn to colour contrasts such as this.

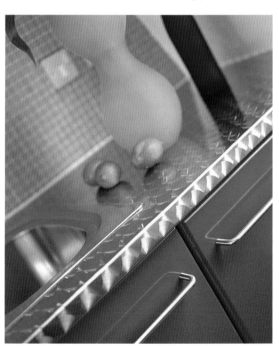

cornflowers

The blue of this daisy-like wildflower is deep and rich in character, but the hint of red some of the flowers contain can make them seem slightly more violet than blue. When this occurs, cornflower blue takes on the gentle, meditative, and soothing qualities of violet.

We absorb colour in many ways – through our eyes, in the food we eat, and through our skin. The bathroom, therefore, is an ideal place to take colour in directly through our naked skin every time we bathe or shower.

A cornflower blue bathroom is perfect for winding down, and soaking in a tub of coloured water is a powerfully direct way of absorbing colour energy. Specialist shops sell colorant for this purpose, but a few drops of organic food dye in the bath water will also work well. Blue's soothing qualities suit an evening bath time.

Soaking in a blue bathroom can recharge the throat chakra. To soothe a sore throat, try laying a blue wash flannel over this area of your body. The throat chakra is connected to expression, creativity, and imagination and so blockages here could eventually lead to difficulties in self-expression, resulting in apathy, withdrawal, and isolation. A blue bath robe worn next to the skin will nourish your body with blue energy. Choose natural fibres and find the particular shade of blue that suits your temperament. Use colourful towels, coloured soaps, and bubble baths to create vibrant, healing colours.

Near right The pure colours in this random mixture of blue mosaic tiles are made richer and more intense when wet. This simulates the sparkling, mottled pools of colour of natural blue lakes and seas.

Middle right For some people, one painted surface provides just the right amount of rich blue colour energy. The clean, white woodwork, bath, and radiator reflect a clear, bright light into this room.

Opposite The warmth of the wooden floor balances the coolness of the blue surroundings. This elegant bathroom makes the perfect setting in which to unwind and relax at the end of a hectic day.

ultramarine

This regal blue, which is very slightly on the red side, is honest and upright. Around the home, such striking intensity is best broken up with white or used in small quantities only, as an accent colour. If tinted with white, ultramarine turns into a gentle sky blue.

Originally, ultramarine pigment was rare and expensive as it was made by grinding down the semiprecious stone lapis lazuli. Nowadays, blue is a popular colour choice. The quickening pace of life means we need to grab whatever free time there is for relaxation and de-stressing ourselves. Strong blues, such as ultramarine, are deeply calming, soothing, and particularly nourishing for those who find it difficult to relax.

However, for the lazy and lethargic, excessive exposure to blue, especially the intense shades, such as the strong ultramarines of the bathrooms shown here, should be avoided. For them, the more uplifting and energizing colours can be a better choice, especially for a morning bath or shower. If your energy levels are already low, too much blue can result in listlessness and inactivity, isolation, and even depression. We are all familiar with the expression "feeling blue". Some types of essentially sad and melancholic music are also referred to as "the Blues". By understanding our attraction to different colours, their strengths and degrees of clarity, we can gain new insights into ourselves.

Near right Mighty strong blues can be too much for some people – this paler, pastel tint is much softer in its effect. We all respond uniquely to the colours around us.

Middle right These ceramic mosaic bathroom tiles share the same intensity of colour as lapis lazuli. The white lines of the grouting break up the the colour effect and help to introduce light into this shower room.

Opposite The intensity of blue in this bathroom is such that it amplifies the illusion of recession that is a common feature of all cool colours. The porcelain bathroom fittings appear clear and bright – whiter than white against this blue.

darkblue

This colour is most effective as part of a decorative scheme when it is teamed with warm colours. As an overall wall colour, however, dark blue is easily overpowering, but if it is applied as an accent colour it can bring a sense of serenity, peace, and calm.

Right Since coloured light has a more powerful effect than coloured pigment, the glowing yellow of this lamp creates a striking contrast with the deeply calming shade of this blue, as well as adding extra lift and warmth to the room.

As blue has a settling effect, so yellow is uplifting. In the bedroom opposite, the yellow tones in the cushions add life and warmth to the room – the blue seems to fix the yellow and hold it in place. To achieve such a dramatic paint colour, you might find it better to use artists' oil, acrylic, and watercolour paints, since many of these contain a richer depth of colour, and are of a much higher quality, than you will find in ordinary household paint. In small areas these colours can be used on top of household paint to produce an especially rich and stunning effect. Try experimenting with this technique directly on a wall, on panels, or even on canvas. Such painted panels in blue are suitable in any tense environment, such as a busy or noisy office. Not only decorative objects in their own right, they can also help to ease the stress of the modern workplace.

Calming blues can be used to good effect in any hectic situation, especially where people seem particularly quick to anger. In public areas, if lengthy queuing is expected – such as in a bank at lunchtime – clear, strong bright blue can act as a salve for fraying tempers.

Left Don't forget to introduce elements of complementary colour into your decorative scheme. These vibrant orange gerberas add an exciting touch of exuberance to this bedroom colour theme, breaking the stillness of the calm, cool wall colour. As dark blue is such a strong hue, small accents, such as the glass vase on the bedside table, are enough to supply a wealth of radiance.

bluesplash

A striking intensity of colour can feel so supportive and nourishing. Just a splash of blue, especially of the richer shades seen here, is often enough in a room setting. The glowing colours of precious blue stone and sapphire are enjoyed in jewel-like proportions.

Blue glass provides a magical colour when illuminated. Blue vases, glasses, or door and wall panels create short bursts of intense blue energy. Coloured glass is so effective that therapists employ it for concentrating the rays used during treatment. This needs to be carried out by a qualified practitioner, however, since adverse effects can result if the timing of a treatment and the use of balancing complementary colours are not properly performed. It is interesting to keep checking your feelings about and responses to different colours, and to look for the reasons why various quantities and strengths of colour seem to

attract you at particular periods or even specific times of the day. The reasons will be very personal – we all respond differently according to our own energy levels, and the colour qualities we possess, need, and attract.

Colour attractions often come and go, so replaceable accessories can serve a useful purpose. A white- or cream-coloured sofa, for example, creates a perfect backdrop for richly coloured cushions that you can easily swap around. Coloured vases, as well as pictures and rugs, provide rich accents without being overpowering.

Near right These cream walls provide a flexible background for changing colour schemes. The strong blue of the cushions is beautifully complemented by the orange in the picture above.

Middle right Position glass objects carefully so that they catch the best of any available light. In this room, the blue glass vase filters sunlight locally as it enters the window, imparting a magical colour to the illumination.

Opposite The strong blue in these pictures is made more vibrant and powerful when seen against the stark white walls and furniture. Being the only colour in this black and white scheme, the blue gains even more impact.

meditative

Violet is the colour most closely associated with a meditative environment. It is a hue to inspire contemplation and introspection and, since it is also the colour of the third eye chakra, violet is intimately connected to intuition, clairvoyance, and psychic opening. Violet helps to develop insight and perception, and it is the colour of dignity and self-respect. Violet's very fine and high vibration makes it an elevating, gentle, and soothing colour.

veryviolet

As an overall wall colour, very violet shades have real impact. Such strength of colour can be suitable for somebody craving the qualities of self-esteem, dignity, and respect. It makes a nourishing, elevating, and inspiring contribution to a home decorative scheme.

Violet is at the opposite end of the visible spectrum to red. And as red has a slow and heavy vibration, so violet is fast and light. Whereas red is related to our physical energy, violet's fine vibration can help lift us up. It is not generally appropriate if you are feeling insecure. This colour often accompanies us at times of spiritual growth and also in our later years. Its elevating qualities can even help to prepare us for when we eventually depart this physical world. In our earlier years, however, we are more likely to be attracted to the colours from the other end of the spectrum, such as reds, oranges, and yellows.

The light, bright window frame in the room opposite acts to break up the expanse of violet walls, while the green foliage seen through the glass in the garden beyond helps to bring about a sense of colour balance. The pure white of the woodwork is fresh in comparison to the violet and also helps to reflect its purity of tone.

Since violet is so light and ethereal in quality, it is well balanced in the room shown below by the solidity and weight of the dark wooden floor and furniture. The wood helps to hold it in place.

Near right If you decide on a powerful wall colour, such as the very violet used here, then keep the ceiling a fresh, bright white and any lamp light simple and clean so that it projects a pure, clear form of illumination.

Middle right Since magenta has the highest and fastest colour vibration, this magenta-coloured sofa adds to the elevating nature of the violet walls – the effect is vibrant and exciting.

Opposite Violet is a contemplative colour, one that encourages you to go within yourself. This room, therefore, can be ideal for yoga, meditation, or other spiritual practices.

deeppurple

This is a profound, rich, regal colour. The strong tones of deep purple carry great impact and create wonderfully intense accents. Just small accessories, such as deep purple cushions on a sofa, add the powerful influence of this colour's energy to a room.

Right The deep colour of the cushion here is almost that of an aubergine. It is heavy and dense, relieved only by the stitched white-and-red pattern. Coarse fabric adds an earthy, grounding quality.

Opposite The slate-gray metal fire surround adds weight and substance to support the sweet, harmonious tones of violet, pink, and blue.

On the colour wheel (*see pp. 8–9*) violet is a secondary colour and it is formed by mixing red and blue pigments. Deep purple hues vary according to the proportions of red and blue they contain. Purple unites the two extremes of the spectrum: red, the energetic stimulator, and blue, a colour with more passive and calming qualities. A purple that contains more red than blue veers toward scarlet, and is heavy and dense as a consequence. If blue predominates, however, the resulting colour is rich and regal.

Colours take on different characteristics when used on different fabrics. A coarse-textured fabric will generally lighten a colour, while a rich, smooth fabric will deepen it. Natural fabrics, such as cotton wool, and silk, enable air and light to flow more freely. Wearing clothes made of these fibres allows colour to pass through more easily and to enter our skin.

In the rooms depicted here, notice that the pink tones in the sofa opposite are slightly on the violet side, and how well they harmonize with the blue seat and violet cushions. To find colour harmonies such as these, look to see which hues sit nearest each other on the colour wheel.

moodindigo

Indigo dye was originally obtained only from the plant world. In its darkest manifestation the depth of this colour can seem impenetrable, and indigo is sometimes compared with the colour of the midnight sky or the very deepest sea.

Some people acknowledge indigo, rather than violet, as the colour of the brow chakra, which governs aspects of insight, intuition, and psychic awareness (*see pp.12–15*). Due to its intensity, indigo is best used in small quantities and in conjunction with lighter colours for support. This treatment can be seen in the room opposite, where the deep, rich colour of the sofa fabric has been balanced by the white walls and ceiling and a large area of window.

Since true indigo is such a dark hue it is best used as an accent colour in a home decorative scheme. If indigo is overused in any one room setting – as an overall wall colour, for example – its intensity can easily become oppressive and subduing.

Indigo is essentially a night-time colour, and so it can be used in a bedroom where it may help to induce restful sleep. But don't forget to work other colours into the scheme to create more light and balance. Different people prefer different strengths of colour, and for a variety of reasons. In general, though, more grounded people can take the best from denser colours.

Near right The weight and solidity of these stones bring a powerful sense of grounding to balance the elevating colours. Strong hues are ideal for small items, such as this shelf, to create accents of intense colour.

Middle right The wonderfully intense violet appears even richer and more magnificent in the living, silky texture of these flower petals. There is no better inspiration for colour than nature.

Opposite The reflective white walls and ceiling of this room create a frame for this sofa. The metallic coloured floor reflects even more light, making the sofa appear to glow in response.

fresh lavender

The protective and antiseptic qualities of the lavender plant have been used for centuries. Lavender brings a beautiful sense of peace and wellbeing. Scent, like colour, represents energy vibrations that are intimately connected with our feelings and emotions.

Right Shiny metal surfaces reflect the maximum amount of light into and around a room. Silvery colours sit particularly well with violet and lavender shades and create an enchanting and elevating atmosphere for this room.

Opposite If a room contains many structural elements, painting them all in the same colour results in a unified and settled type of effect. In this room, the brickwork, wooden steps, the mezzanine bed, and even the pipes are all painted in an identical shade of gentle lavender.

In addition to the fragrance, the colour we call lavender also takes its name from the beautiful garden perennial shrub *Lavandula*. And just as the fragrance is rich, delicate, and tranquil, so, too, are the visual attributes most closely associated with the colour.

Lavender has a pale, blue tone. It is light and ethereal in quality, projecting a fine and delicate vibration. For those who prefer the pastel hues, lavender has a delicate hint of violet about it. Some people find that being surrounded by strong, vibrant colours feels like being shouted at. Those with a more gentle disposition often prefer to have more gentle tones in their homes. Too much intensity of any one hue can tip the scales in favour of the negative side, which is an aspect of all the spectral colours, especially when not compensated for with opposite colours.

Be careful when using lavender in any rooms of the home that do not receive much natural light – in deep shadow, it can take on a rather gray-looking appearance. Lavender tends to work best when teamed with white – an example of which you can see opposite.

Lavender, like violet, is a colour to bolster your self-esteem, and so you may want to try it in or around your dressing area, where it may help you to feel happy with your appearance. Try wearing lavender if you are feeling less than confident with your looks for some reason. Used in the bedroom, it can soothe the mind and so encourage restful, refreshing sleep.

lilactime

Lilac is a sweet and gentle version of violet. Slightly more pink than blue in content, lilac is a fragrant, delicate, active, and extremely attractive hue. For those drawn to the lighter pastel colours, lilac can be a rewarding, if perhaps temporary, choice of colour.

Changing the decorative scheme of your home is a major step, so, until you feel certain about committing yourself, it may be a good idea to introduce new colours through small, replaceable items, such as a tablecloth, painted table top, vase, or perhaps a chair. Painting just one wall in a colour such as lilac can be very effective and easily repainted if you do not like the effect. Colour attractions can be very temporary in nature, and you will need to guard against expensive and disruptive mistakes, and are especially connected to the violet area of the spectrum, including lilac. It is a valuable colour when your sense of

self-worth needs a boost or your self-esteem is at a low ebb. Exercise caution, however, for once your circumstances change and your mood improves, you may find that your liking for lilac has somewhat cooled.

A lilac-coloured blind at the window in the room shown below acts as a filter, absorbing all other colour energies and allowing only pinky-blue light to pass through to create a calming and tranquil atmosphere. Your clothes act in much the same way, permitting only certain colour energies to reach your body.

Near right Lilac-coloured blinds glow in the sunshine, bathing the whole room in glorious, morale-boosting light. Luscious green foliage in the garden beyond supports the colour well.

Middle right In this kitchen, painting one wall lilac produces just enough impact. As it is, the white retains a light and clear reflection.

Opposite Pieces of coloured furniture can be moved from room to room to keep decorative schemes fresh and alive. The round table and the curves of this chair break up and balance the hard, straight lines of the room, which, otherwise, could be too enclosing and restrictive in character.

purplehaze

Purple colours are powerful, dramatic, and mystical. In this living room, a haze of purple produces a dignified space for retreat and introspection – an enclosed refuge, somewhere to rest, a place to go within, to listen to music, to contemplate.

Purple is not an easy colour to wear, so you may want to compensate for this by integrating it into a decorative theme somewhere in your home. Purple, however, should not be your first choice for busy, active rooms, such as a kitchen, as it discourages physical work and can encourage dreaminess. Depending on the mood you want, though, purple may be fine in a study, for bringing out the intuitive side of your nature, but balance it with some yellow to sharpen the intellect. Because it brings such a strong sense of dignity, purple can be a helpful colour to have around you when you are feeling ill or helpless.

These darker violet tones bring with them a range of connotations. Purple, for example, is a sign of rank in some religious orders. It also has regal and royal associations, making it aloof, refined, and majestic – perhaps even a little pompous at times. Purple's complementary colour is yellow. These two colours contrast both in appearance and in character – purple relating to intuition and yellow to intellect. Placed side by side, purple and yellow make a dazzling combination, but small splashes of one near a main scheme of the other results in balance and harmony.

Near right These yellow pots leap out of the frame when seen contrasting with the purple walls of this room. Like two opposing characters, the colours work to exaggerate each other's differences.

Middle right This silver-coloured mirror frame adds to the elevating nature of the purple walls, while the pale floor and fire surround lighten and balance the atmosphere.

Opposite Painting everything above the picture rail in white keeps this room looking clean and bright, and prevents the strength of the purple becoming oppressive. The large area of window allows plenty of sunlight into the room making it airy and cheerful.

romantic

Pink is the colour that is probably most closely associated with love and romance. It is gentle and soothing, and an extremely feminine colour. The warm and caressing shades of pink are caring and affectionate. Pink is, like green, sometimes seen as the colour of the heart chakra (*see pp. 12–15*). It is the nurturing colour of love and self-love, and is tender, protective, and full of compassion. Pink is the gentle colour of love.

shockingpink

Shocking pinks are vivid, dramatic, and exciting hues that sometimes appear to glitter and sparkle, and the atmosphere they generate is hot and lively . . . even daring. Elements of shocking pink are all you need to bring a sense of fun, movement, and light.

Whether you are looking for a colour theme that is a celebration of love and affection or one that is uplifting, exciting, and energizing, shocking pink may be able to satisfy your needs.

Romantic colour schemes can, on the one hand, be extravagant, moody, and sentimental expressions of personality, while, on the other, they can be used more simply around the home – in ways that are neither wild nor far fetched. The term "in the pink", for example, implies all is well, healthy, and rosy.

Since shocking pink is so strong and powerful, it is more effective when used in small quantities, supplying controlled bursts of energy. Four shocking pink walls are too much for most people, so it is best to temper the colour's abundant vivacity with plenty of white.

People vary in their preferences for pink, with some being more colour sensitive than others. Children often adore the colour pink, but in general they react more quickly than adults to colour and so in therapy treatments they receive a lighter and briefer dose of colour energy.

Near right When using exciting and lively colours together, such as the magenta, orange, and gold in this cushion, an expanse of white provides the perfect background against which to see them in their full glory.

Middle right The undersides of these wall-mounted shelves have been painted in blocks of vibrant colour. This has transformed a very utilitarian arrangement into an eye-catching room feature.

Opposite For dramatic effect, this is hard to beat. By dressing the windows in sheer pink curtain fabric the room is flooded with colour energy every time the sun shines.

sugarcandy

Sugar pink is sweet and pure, feminine and gentle, and soft and loving. However, if it is over-represented in any one room, like too much candy it can be rather sickly. This pink is probably best used to moderate the harder, colder effect of the more masculine colours.

Right This headboard can be re-covered time and time again to suit different colour themes, styles, and moods, so why not let your imagination run wild when it comes to creating exciting and colourful patterns? Without the blue of the cupboards and floor, however, this amount of pink can quickly become overpowering.

Opposite Too much of any hot and stimulating colour in a bedroom can be disturbing to the point where your sleep is interrupted. But the splashes of red in this bedroom simply add an extra touch of heat and passion to the gentler qualities of the larger areas of pink.

These pinks are often avoided because they are associated with fussy patterns or overly sweet and sugary tones that come across as false or artificial. It is important to check your personal reactions to colours to discover why you have problems enjoying their positive qualities.

Although pink is essentially a pale form of red, made by mixing red and white together, it produces a very different type of energy. The addition of white brings lighter, less heavy qualities. Whereas red is considered a masculine colour, pink is a distinctly feminine one. Pink is much less aggressive than red, less physical, and less primal. Just as red is a warm colour so is pink, but it is gently stimulating rather than fiery in temperament.

In the bedroom opposite, various pinks have been combined to create horizontal blocks of colour. For a harmonious colour theme, buy paint corresponding to the darkest hue, such as the deep magenta bands, and then add increasing quantities of white to produce a gradation of paler tints. Some vertically striped patterns can feel discordant; but horizontal stripes, such as those used on the right, generally have a more calming effect.

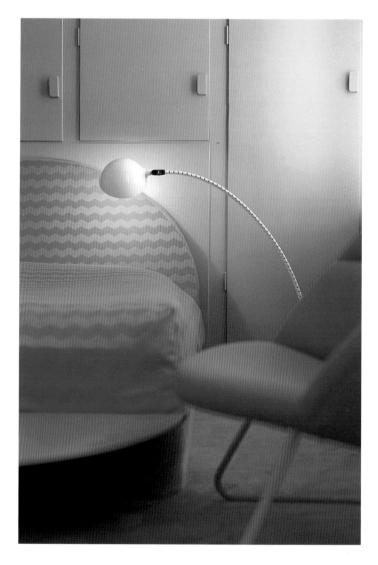

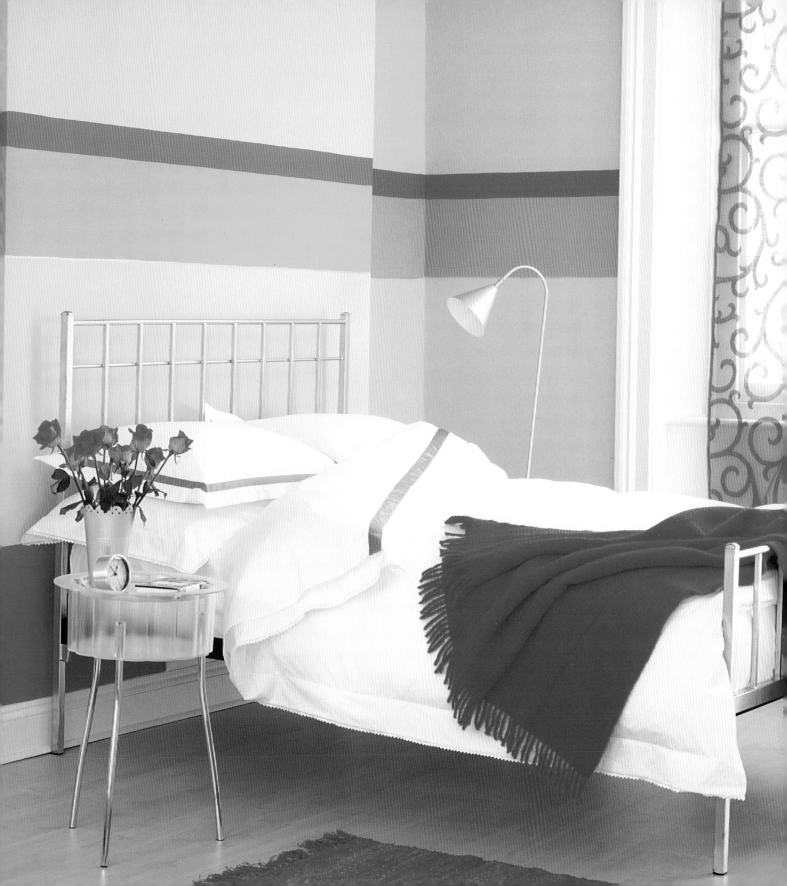

rose-tinted

The expression "looking through rose-tinted spectacles" implies a biased, overly optimistic view of life – a beautifully romantic quality. Rose tints are gentle, subtle pastel colours of delicate pink encompassing the softer qualities of this colour.

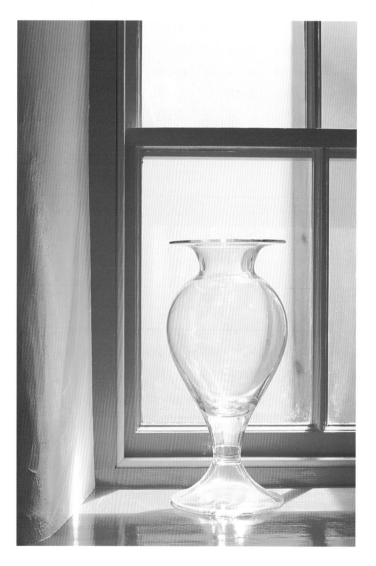

Red sits between orange and violet on the colour wheel, so the colour pink can be influenced either by pale orange and become a peachy pink, or by the violet side and become more of a mauve-pink. Each type of pink has its own energy signature. Mauve-pinks are generally calm colours because of the influence of the blue; peachy pinks, however, tend to be more stimulating and cheerful. Complementaries vary, depending on the type of pink involved, but they are generally in the range of pale green to turquoise. As with all decorative schemes, introducing touches of the main colour's complementary helps to create balance and harmony.

Warm peach-like tones of pink can be very flattering – some people claim that painting a room in this colour can take years off their complexion. It also creates a cosy, active, and inviting atmosphere.

Lighting is important. Diffused light is subtle and intimate, and rose-tinted light is gentle and soothing to the heart. There is no light to compare with the warm and golden flame of a candle. Like sunshine itself, this flame is natural and contains all the colours of the spectrum.

Opposite Don't overlook some very simple lighting tricks, such as carefully positioning glass objects to catch and filter sunlight as it enters a room. Here, the glass vase reflects the sunlight right across the room to produce a dazzling and sparkling effect.

Left Use different coloured lighting to modify a room's atmosphere to suit your mood. These coloured lights give off a soft, rose-pink glow when seen against the clear white wall. And the effect is gentle, soothing, and very romantic.

ROMANTIC

magenta-pink

More forceful pinks are bright, vibrant, and joyous colours. They can also be very soothing and gentle, and warm and affectionate. When used around the home, these colours can be positive and reassuring, and they have protective influences.

Magenta-pink is considered to be the eighth colour of the spectrum, the colour with the highest and fastest vibration. It is formed when violet and red light are mixed, and it is the colour of the crown chakra – the centre of understanding, cognition, and wisdom. Magenta-pink encourages introspection and it can help to steady overactive behaviour. It also has the energy to transform and release, and thus induce change. This is a colour for moving on and letting go of things. Splashes of magenta bring a special freshness to life and have a spiritual and uplifting quality. Around the home this colour is best used in smaller quantities or combined with paler, softer pinks, or its complementary colour, green.

An interesting exercise is to ask yourself which colour for you is fun, happy, sad, serious, friendly, lonely, and so on. Then ask yourself which colour you have most of, less of, wear most often, or avoid or never use. Doing this can help you introduce new colour influences into your life. We may not recognize it but the colours of your clothes, for example, are a sub-conscious reflection of your feelings and moods. By becoming more aware of colours – in your home, of your clothes,

in your general environment – you can appreciate the various energies that they supply and start to use them to create the environment that is most supportive for you as an individual or for the needs of your family or loved ones.

Right Paper lanterns are a simple, inexpensive, and fun way to introduce coloured light into your home. These lanterns are most often made in the clean, clear, and bright colours with which children usually love to surround themselves.

Opposite The accents of gray/blue tones in this room help to support, balance, and contain the very active and hot neighbouring colours. Prominent splashes of these vibrant pink tones can have a powerful impact on mood.

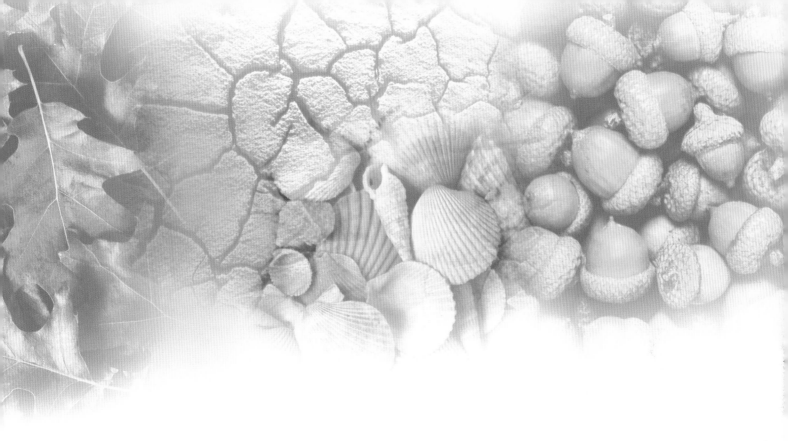

grounded

Brown is the most grounding of all the colours. The influence of this colour helps to bring us down to earth and to make us feel rooted and connected with the physical world that surrounds us. The earth supplies us with a constant force of energy, and consciously bringing this into our homes can assist us in feeling supported and stronger in ourselves. Nature supplies us with unlimited sources of this colour inspiration.

woodtones

Using wood in its natural state is the easiest way to introduce shades of brown into your home. No matter how dark wood tones become, even when they verge on black, you can always see movement, light, and pattern beneath the surface.

Right The rich, rosy chestnut tones of this wood-lined corridor make the space look warm and welcoming. Recessed spotlighting has been carefully positioned to highlight key features, such as the wall painting, while the light creams in the neighbouring room keeps this connecting space bright and airy.

Opposite Light and creamy colours in this room work to prevent the brown tones from becoming overly dominant. The unusual lamp, which is an immediate focal point, adds its own interest to the scheme, creating yet more exciting texture.

The natural colours of wood range from the soft blonde of pine to the deep, dark shades of mahogany – and no two wood tones are ever quite the same. All cultures treasure the unique beauty of natural wood and having wooden doors, window frames, tables, chairs, floors, walls, and ceilings are just some of the ways you can enjoy the supportive quality of brown colour energy without resorting to the often heavy and oppressive opaqueness of brown pigment. But every colour has to be used with care and restraint, and too much brown in the home can feel restricting and limiting. In excess, the solidness of brown can hold you back from change and progress.

In these rooms, wood is featured in the ceiling and as wall panels and flooring. All of these surfaces can be treated with varnish but the best effects are often achieved by using natural waxes that soak into the wood. As flooring, wood is warm and welcoming to the touch. Like the colour of the soil, a natural wooden floor makes us feel supported and secure. Bear in mind, however, that floors that are too light in colour can create the opposite effect – making us feel insecure and unsupported.

autumnhues

Autumn hues are inviting, deep, and rich, and they are particularly cosy and comforting during the colder seasons. The warmer colours of the spectrum – the reds, oranges, and yellows – create the most sympathetic associations with these burnt and russet hues.

Browns in nature are most often broken and variegated. Like the grain of wood, this adds light and movement to the colour. In the home, brown is solid and substantial, strong, sound, and reliable. It is steady and grounding. There are many tones of brown, but traditionally brown is formed by mixing yellow, red, and black. Brown is the colour of commitment and security. People who are attracted to brown tend to be committed, trustworthy, hard-working, practical, and reliable. In the 1940s, brown was a popular colour to wear to work, and brown suits, dresses, jackets, and coats were very fashionable. At that time people were also commonly committed to their workplace, often staying in one job for life. Now, lifestyles have changed and brown is less fashionable. The gray and charcoal colours of today reflect a more neutral, less committed attitude.

The sky blue elements in the room opposite add balance and a sense of openness and expansion when viewed against the solidity of the brown. This shade of blue also contrasts well with the brickwork, enhancing its complementary orange tones.

Near right The luxurious velvet texture of this cushion fabric adds a sumptuous quality and depth of colour to this rich autumnal chestnut hue.

Middle right Unusual fabrics can make interesting throws and cushions. The fake fur and sandy suede textures used here are lifted by the background of a clean white sofa.

Opposite Cleaned up bare brickwork can make a wonderful room feature. The brickwork revealed on this chimney breast has a mottled finish that is subtle yet has plenty of visual interest. Sealing the bricks makes cleaning them easier and it can also enhance their naturally warm and gentle colours.

softstone

Earthenware, ceramics, stones, granite, and even bare plaster walls are just some of the ways to bring the tones of natural stone into your home. Although not nourishing, as are the rainbow colours, they have a vital role in supporting and grounding the others.

In most situations, it is best to use the soft hues of natural stone alongside a traditional range of decorative colours. Too many of these stone colours used alone and unrelieved can feel flat and neutral, and perhaps a little dull. However, look closely at a piece of polished marble or granite, for example, or at a square-cut face of sandstone, and you will see that they contain a surprisingly wide range of subtle tones. To enjoy these in your own home is not difficult – irregular pieces of faceted slate or smooth, water-worn pebbles make excellent door stops or other decorative objects.

An attraction to very dull, flat colours indicates an insecurity related to the aspects of the particular colours involved. However, an attraction to a clear, bright colour denotes a clarity concerning the issues and statements associated with that colour. An attraction to pure, clear green, for example, can be related to confidence and healing connected to issues of the heart. By analysing the colours we choose to have around us we can learn a great deal about ourselves. The more we see particular colours, the more they can be seen as messengers and reflections of our inner nature.

Right The soft pebble-coloured walls of this room are lifted by a large panel of pure white pigment. This contrast helps to enliven the stone colours, preventing them from appearing too flat, and it also brings life and extra light to the room.

Opposite The hues of this room result from leaving the plastered walls in a natural, untreated state. Unpainted plaster stays porous, allowing air to pass freely so that the surface can "breathe". If you like, try polishing plaster with natural waxes to deepen its colour and produce a lustrous sheen. The golden fabrics of these cushions add a sense of light and sparkle to this room's scheme.

dustybrown

As they most often appear in nature, shades of dusty brown are best used in the home in broken patterns, combined with other colour rather than alone. In granite, marble, and wood, the warm hues of dusty brown form beautiful natural patterns.

Right Wood is a healthy, living material; it is organic and supportive and has the ability to recharge your batteries. When natural, untreated wood becomes wet it has its own, very beautiful, soothing, and gentle aroma.

If you are planning on making a change to the decorative scheme in your home, it is important to check your responses to the different tones and shades of any particular colour you may be thinking of using – just a fraction lighter or darker can change its whole character and therefore radically alter the effect it may have on you.

Before deciding on a new colour, such as the dusty brown shown here, try living with a large sample of it first. View this sample under the types of lighting, both artificial and natural, that occur normally in the room. You may find that throughout the day there is a difference between what feels grounded and supportive and what feels murky and dull.

The marble in this bathroom is wonderfully symbolic of the solidity and weight of the earth. Brown-coloured flooring or wooden floorboards and carpets can help you feel the grounding energy of this colour. Having wooden slats in the bathroom to step on to from the bath can also create the same feeling, especially because of the direct contact with your bare feet.

Left The marble used in this bathroom projects a strong sense of weight and solidity. The room benefits from high levels of natural light and this, combined with the white walls and ceiling, prevents the decorative stone from feeling too heavy and overbearing.

quietgray

The quiet, more laid-back shades of gray are often best used to support and assist hues from other parts of the spectrum, rather than featuring in their own right. The neutrality and tranquillity of gray exerts a steadying influence on the more vibrant colours.

Including different textures and natural fibres in your home, or as a part of your clothing, can be important elements in creating a well-grounded scheme. Wool and leather are particularly related to our physical nature and are, in effect, grounding materials. Gentle, subtle tones of gray are found in many natural materials. In the home, these coverings can be used as, say, rugs, or as furniture fabrics and throws, cushions covers, and so on. Gray tones are used most effectively in the home when they are placed to steady and back-up other, more vibrant colours that, without this unique and neutral support,

can feel too loud or uncontained. All colours benefit from the presence of gray. A world without the quiet shades of gray can come across as lacking in structure, sustenance, and support.

The pale wooden floors and white bed linen used in the room opposite make it light and clear – too many darker tones can become fixing and heavy. If gray is allowed to predominate it may make you feel rather uncommitted, which can lead on to feelings of fear and negativity and so it needs to be balanced with lighter, brighter colours.

Near right These rustic, leafy themes are gentle and supportive reminders of nature. Use the lighter shades of gray for a more tranquil effect.

Middle right Woollen-textured throws and blankets are comforting and grounding. Natural pigments produce subtle hues, such as you can see in these cool, neutral, and quiet stony grays.

Opposite The solidity and strength of a headboard such as this help you feel supported and secure. As grays are tranquil, they encourage peaceful, restful sleep, but the addition of the purer rainbow colours can make your sleep more nourishing and replenishing.

directory

The study of colour has been of great fascination to many people throughout the ages. One of the leading pioneers of modern day colour therapy is Theo Gimbel of Hygeia Studios. He started with his research in 1956 and his was the very first centre teaching and treating with colour. The majority of colour practitioners have been taught by him. His years of study and research into colour have helped to make such an immense subject more accessible to many people.

Opposite are some addresses of associations and centres teaching colour therapy:

COLOUR THERAPY ASSOCIATION
P O Box 309
Camberley
Surrey GU15 2LE
Tel: 01276 682113

HYGEIA COLLEGE OF COLOUR THERAPY
Brook House
Avening
Tetbury
Glos GL8 8NS
Tel: 01453 832150
email:hygeiathg@netscapeonline.co.uk
Principal: Theo Gimbel

INTERNATIONAL ASSOCIATION OF COLOUR
46 Cottenham Road
Histon
Camb CB4 9ES
Tel: 01223 563403
email: michael@kgrevis.freeserve.co.uk
Principal: Michael Grevis

IRIS INTERNATIONAL
Farfields House
Jubilee Road
Totnes
Devon TQ9 5BP
Tel: 01803 868037
email:irisint@eclipse.co.uk
Principal: Suzy Chiazzari

KNOW YOURSELF THROUGH COLOUR FOUNDATION
5 Church Walk
Worthing
West Sussex BN11 2LS
Tel: 01903 216311
Principal: Marie Louise Lacy

LIVING COLOUR
P O Box 27016
London N2 0ZA
Tel: 0208 883 4988
www.living-colour.co.uk
Principals: Howard and Dorothy Sun

ANN LLOYD
8 Rosslyn Hill
Hampstead
London NW3 1PH
Tel: 0207 794 7064

SCHOOL OF MANTRACOLOUR HEALING
35 Chelsea Manor Court
Flood Street
London SW3 5SB
Tel: 0207 385 1525
Mobile: 07973 315 950
email: deborah@mantracolour.freeserve.co.uk
Principal: Deborah Italiano

index

acknowledgments

The author would like to thank Selina Mumford, Judith More, Janis Utton, Emily Asquith, Jonathan Hilton, and everybody involved in producing this book.

Many thanks go to Deborah Italiano of MantraColour Healing for reading through the text and making very helpful comments.

Thank you to all the colour schools and practitioners working to bring a new awareness of colour into every aspect of our lives.

Picture credits

Arcaid / Petrina Tinslay/Belle 87 / Richard Bryant 123; **Axiom Photographic Agency /** James Morris 36, 44 right, 80 right, 82 right, 83 / Luke White 64 left & right, 65; **Mark Brazier Jones** 109; **Richard Glover** 67; **Robert Harding Picture Library /** GE Magazines Ltd 2, 38, 39, 98 right, 107, 122 left; **Interior Archive /** Fernando Bengoechea (owner: Liz O'Brien) 26 left, (property: South Beach) 52 left / Simon Brown (designer: Conran) 86 left, (owner: Rebecca Hossack) 94 left, (designer: Margaret Howell) 122 right, (stylist: Melanie Molesworth) 94 right, (designer: Clodagh Nolan) 85; **Inside Stock Image Production /** House & Leisure Magazine 6 / House & Leisure Magazine/G McAllister 30, 31; **Jonathan Pilkington** (designer: Johnny Moke) 57; **Simon Upton** (theatre director: Frank McGuiness) 81, (designer: Miller Miller) 95; **Andrew Wood** (florist: Paula Pryke) 66, (architect: Mike Tonkin) 26 right; **IPC International Syndications** Country Homes & Interiors/Spike Powell 19; **Ray Main/ Mainstream** front cover, back cover, 24 left & right, 25, 28, 29, 32, 33, 40 top, 41, 45, 46 left, 47, 48, 49, 53, 54 right, 55 right, 60, 61, 71, 72, 73, 76, 79, 80 left, 86 right, 92, 93, 104 left & right, 105, 108, 110, 111, (designer: Nick Allen) 82 left, (architect: Duncan Baker Brown) 56, (designer: Nana Ditzel) front cover top left, 106, (designer: Oriana Fielding Banks) 119, (architect: Granit Architects) 78, (designer: Lawrence Llewelyn-Bowen) 77, (architect: Andrew Martin) 52 right, 54 left, 99, Martin Lec Associates 46 right, Mathmos 90 left & right, 91, (designer: Roger Oates) 27, (designer: Drew Plunkett) 68; **Octopus Publishing Group /** Dominic Blackmore front cover top right, 37, 40 below, 42, 59, 70, 114, 115, 118, 120 / Gary Latham 13, 14 / Neil Mersh 116, 117 / Steve Tanner 20 / Simon Upton 4; **David Parmiter** 98 left, 100, 101; View 58, Architect: Simon Conder Associates; 69 / Nick Hulton 43; **Elizabeth Whiting and Associates /** Rodney Hyett 44 left / Mark Thomas 96